AF338299

MARTIN BUCER

CASCADE COMPANIONS

The Christian theological tradition provides an embarrassment of riches: from Scripture to modern scholarship, we are blessed with a vast and complex theological inheritance. And yet this feast of traditional riches is too frequently inaccessible to the general reader.

The Cascade Companions series addresses the challenge by publishing books that combine academic rigor with broad appeal and readability. They aim to introduce nonspecialist readers to that vital storehouse of authors, documents, themes, histories, arguments, and movements that comprise this heritage with brief yet compelling volumes.

MARTIN BUCER

An Introduction to His Life and Theology

DONALD K. MCKIM
JIM WEST

Foreword by
Jon Balserak

CASCADE *Books* · Eugene, Oregon

MARTIN BUCER
An Introduction to His Life and Theology

Cascade Companions

Cascade Books
An Imprint of Wipf and Stock Publishers
199 W. 8th Ave., Suite 3
Eugene, OR 97401

www.wipfandstock.com

PAPERBACK ISBN: 978-1-6667-3898-8
HARDCOVER ISBN: 978-1-6667-3899-5
EBOOK ISBN: 978-1-6667-3900-8

Cataloguing-in-Publication data:

Names: McKim, Donald K. [author]. | West, Jim [author] | Balserak, Jon [foreword writer]

Title: Martin Bucer : an introduction to his life and theology / Donald K. McKim and Jim West.

Description: Eugene, OR: Cascade Books, 2023 | Series: Cascade Companions | Includes bibliographical references.

Identifiers: ISBN 978-1-6667-3898-8 (paperback) | ISBN 978-1-6667-3899-5 (hardcover) | ISBN 978-1-6667-3900-8 (ebook)

Subjects: LCSH: Bucer, Martin, 1491–1551 | Reformed Church—South Germany | Reformation | Theology, Doctrinal—History—16th century

Classification: BR350.B93 M35 2023 (print) | BR350.B93 (ebook)

We wish to thank Springer Nature for permission to quote from N. Scott Amos's *Bucer's Prefatory Lectures on Ephesians and His Use of Biblical Humanist Theological Method*, 2015.

To the memory of David F. Wright
To all the readers of this book
May they learn appreciatively from Martin Bucer
about Christian faith and life

CONTENTS

FOREWORD

THE IDEA THAT MARTIN Bucer's work and writings would require introduction in the twenty-first century would, I suspect, have astonished his sixteenth-century contemporaries. Bucer was, after all, a superb scholar, theologian, humanist, biblical exegete, and reformer. His conversion to Protestantism had produced a Christian of exemplary character, who profoundly influenced his age. He was learned, devout, and a prolific writer. Yet here we are.

We might muse, briefly, on the contemporary neglect of Bucer. When modern scholars began their work of producing critical editions and their translation projects, why did they overlook him? There are, of course, some examples of work on Bucer. Constantin Hopf, Robert Stupperich, Willem Van 't Spijker, Wilhelm Neuser, Peter Matheson, and Amy Nelson Burnett were among the (small) collection of scholars in the twentieth century who devoted their energies to him. They generally wrote monographs and articles; meanwhile Martin Greschat produced the seminal biography of Bucer in 1990.[1] Pierre Fraenkel and Irena Backus are among those who worked on critical editions of some of Bucer's writings.[2] The work of translating Bucer was

1. Greschat, *Martin Bucer.*
2. *Martini Buceri Opera.*

slower in coming. P. T. Fuhrmann's little book *Instruction in Love, by Martin Bucer, the Reformer* appeared in 1952 (this translation was reprinted fairly recently). Wilhelm Pauck produced a translation of Bucer's *De Regno Christi* for the Library of Christian Classics series. And David F. Wright published a superb edition entitled *Common Places of Martin Bucer* in 1972. Meanwhile, the corpora of Martin Luther and John Calvin were the focus of massive amounts of attention and volumes introducing Luther and Calvin to lay audiences are numerous. Why such a stark difference? Was it national interest? In the case of Luther, perhaps. This seems a less likely explanation for Calvin. Whatever the case, it is a privilege to have the opportunity to write this foreword introducing this volume—one that is so needed for a figure so important.

Some predecessors to this volume exist. David Steinmetz's *Reformers in the Wings* comes to mind as it contains a short chapter on Bucer. Likewise, Ian Hazlett's chapter on Bucer in *The Cambridge Companion to Reformation Theology* can be mentioned.[3] But none of these does what Don McKim and Jim West's superb book, which you hold in your hand, does. Steinmetz's little chapter focuses primarily on his life, while Hazlett's focuses on the man's theology. Both are brief, hampered by the constraints of short chapters. The present volume is considerably larger and more substantial than either of the aforementioned treatments, while still being pocket-sized.

McKim and West are both scholarly and gifted at making ideas clear. These dual qualities have led to the production of a superb piece of work. During their careers, both men have written on a wide range of subjects, including recently publishing an introduction similar to this one on

3. Hazlett, "Bucer," in *The Cambridge Companion to Reformation Theology*, 100–112.

the great Swiss reformer Heinrich Bullinger—a reformer, intriguingly, who had his run-ins with Martin Bucer, as West and McKim note in their exceptional biography of Bucer with which this volume begins.

Although he engaged in disputes with Bullinger and others, Bucer was known for his irenicism. While not unique among his contemporaries, Bucer's irenic disposition was unusual. One thinks of the near-perpetual polemic that figures like Luther, Thomas Müntzer, Andreas Bodenstein von Karlstadt, and Huldrych Zwingli engaged in. Their arguments with one another and with Anabaptists and other groups were characterized by belligerence and, particularly in the case of Luther, foul-mouthed insults. The sixteenth century was certainly not known for producing mealy-mouthed voices. Yet Bucer stands in distinction to these more aggressive reformers, making him a remarkably appropriate addition to our age—an age during which arguing belligerently over social media with little concern for whom one harms has become commonplace and insidious.

Not much (if anything) about his upbringing or early life might lead one to guess he would have been an irenicist. Born in 1491, Bucer entered the Dominican order in 1507 or possibly 1508 at Sélestat. The great change that occurred in Bucer's life came when, in April 1518, he heard Luther explain and defend his theology at the Heidelberg Disputation. Moved by what he witnessed, Bucer would leave the order, settling in Strasbourg in 1523. He married in 1524. He became an important reformer and theological voice and labored against Roman Catholics as well as Anabaptists and others. He was present at the Marburg Colloquy in 1529. He established the *Collegium praedicatorum* in 1534 for the training of ministers for the church. He was friendly with and worked with Philip Melanchthon, Johannes Gropper, Johannes Sturm, and other major theological figures.

The upheaval introduced by the Augsburg Interim of 1548 meant that Bucer could no longer stay in the Emperor Charles V's territory, and so he went to England at Thomas Cranmer's invitation, settling in Cambridge. He worked there for several years, dying in early 1551. A productive life, one cannot help but wonder: had Bucer been able to stay in Strasbourg and establish himself even more firmly there in the manner of Calvin in Geneva or Bullinger in Zurich, might he possibly have been better known today?

Bucer is famous (or infamous) for being diplomatic and willing to engage in compromise in order to make progress. This has been interpreted variously by contemporaries as well as by modern scholars. To some, he is regarded as an opportunist, insincere, malleable, and untrustworthy. Others regard him as shrewd, practical, sensible. In a world full of moral complexity, Bucer managed himself and his theological projects with some care. His training as a Dominican surely introduced him to the Catholic moral tradition and to principles that help one to navigate a morally complex world—principles that involve varying degrees of cooperation with sin and evil. One thinks, for instance, of the (so-called) doctrine of double-effect. Thomas Aquinas discusses this in his *Summa Theologica* II-II Q64 section 7, where in the *respondeo* he declares: "Nothing hinders one act from having two effects only one of which is intended, while the other is beside the intention."[4] Aquinas addresses this in relation to the question of whether one may ever kill someone else in self-defense. Wherever he learned it from, Bucer's capacity for making decisions that exhibited a degree of moral subtlety (some would say equivocation) is known, being illustrated perhaps most clearly in his

4. "Respondeo dicendum quod nihil prohibet unius actus esse duos effectus, quorum alter solum sit in intentione, alius vero sit praeter intentionem" (Aquinas, *Summa Theologica* , II-II Q64, s.7).

well-known decision to approve Philip of Hesse's bigamous marriage.

Although he could occasionally be stubborn, Bucer was also known for his pacific disposition. Calvin, for instance, who lived in Strasbourg from late-1538 to 1541, regarded him as a father in the faith and held him in the highest regard. Bucer could still, that said, hold a firm line in the face of pressure from others. Bucer took a gradual approach to the reformation of Europe. This meant that, for example, his attitude towards Nicodemism was discernibly different from that of someone like Calvin, who was intense in his opposition to it. Thus, when, in the mid-1540s, Bucer was requested by Calvin (in response to a complaint by Antoine Fumée) to produce a piece of guidance intended for French evangelicals regarding whether they must decide never to attend Roman Catholic Mass opting instead to flee France in order to worship rightly (in a Reformed church in Geneva or elsewhere)—to depart as Abram had been commanded to do by God in Genesis 12:1—the response from Bucer was gentle and encouraging. He urged the French believers, likely to Calvin's great frustration, that anything in the ordinary service of worship that was from God such as the ordinary readings, sermons, and the like could not be so severely corrupted that the godly believer could be kept from hearing and sensing the Lord acting for the increase of their own growth in godliness.[5] This was Bucer's gentleness on display; his high regard for the things the Lord could do, and was doing, in his church even despite the intrusion of human ceremonies. And this gentleness is what appears in West and McKim's superb volume. That being so, the Bucer

---

5. D. F. Wright, "Why Was Calvin So Severe a Critic of Nicodemism?" in Wright, Lane, and Balserak, eds., *Calvinus Evangelii Propugnator*, 66–90; esp. 78–80, contra Carlos Eire, *War against the Idols*, 247 n.51.

presented here is not idolized; his flaws are apparent and admirably discussed by McKim and West.

This volume presents its readers with the life and theology of a figure profoundly important for Protestant theology and for understanding and living the Christian life. It provides readers with a fine treatment that does a superb job of setting Bucer into his sixteenth-century context. It exhibits an expansive knowledge of Bucer's times and corpus—and also an expansive knowledge of those with whom Bucer interacted. With his context set in place, the volume works through major theological topics. It covers his views on Scripture. It covers his understanding of the members of the Trinity. It treats Bucer's soteriology, the church, sacraments, and last things. Concerning all these topics, the coverage is marvelously accessible while also clearly being the production of two superb scholarly minds.

As one would expect from two scholars with such concern for the church and for their readers, the volume ends with a chapter considering Bucer's significance. Thus, the book you have in your hands is a valuable one. I commend it to you in the strongest possible terms. It is a superb introduction to an extremely important individual.

Jon Balserak
Bristol, England

PREFACE

WHEN WE FINISHED OUR volume on Bullinger, we had had such a wonderful experience together that we were keen to write something again. We pondered several possibilities and finally landed on a volume on Martin Bucer. Our reasons for doing so were very simple: Bucer, like Bullinger, is fairly well known among Reformation scholars but hardly known at all among Reformed Christians. We wanted to remedy, so far as we could, this shortfall.

Martin Bucer was a complex, multilayered, profoundly significant theologian, pastor, and scholar. But his works have scarcely seen the light of day in English. Very few of his works have been translated. Very few outside academia read him. And few have heard of him. Yet in his day, among his peers and colleagues, he was widely respected in many corners of non-Roman Catholic European Christianity. His friends and admirers included Calvin and Bullinger as well as Melanchthon and even Martin Luther.

Bucer was also tremendously influential in his efforts to unite the various factions of Lutherans and Reformed and even hard-core Zwinglians. He failed, for many reasons, most of which will be examined in due course. But the primary reason was because too many of the first-generation

Reformers were deeply suspicious of one another and pro-foundly stubborn.

So, we thought, we should write a book very much like the book we penned concerning Heinrich Bullinger. We think the English-speaking world would benefit by knowing this conciliatory man in a time when fractures and divisions are dividing families and churches and even peoples. Bucer brings with him a spirit of compassionate respect and deep appreciation for the truths others hold. Perhaps just a portion of his cloak might fall on contemporary Western Christianity. If that were to happen because people knew more of this great man and came to understand the virtue of honest, truth-bearing compromise, then we would consider this book a tremendous success. We have greatly enjoyed this joint-venture into Martin Bucer and hope this book will be a helpful introduction to this great soul.

Donald K. McKim, Germantown, Tennessee
Jim West, Petros Tennessee
May, 2022

ACKNOWLEDGMENTS

The writing of a book is never an individual enterprise. Even if one is a single author, all who write are dependent on the ones who come before and who stand beside us.

Don would like to thank Jim for all his kindness and sharing his considerable gifts in our crafting of this book. It is truly a joy to work with such a competent, kind, theologian and friend. And Jim would like to express his thanks to Don for his cordiality, wisdom, wit, and expertise.

Don also thanks LindaJo, his wife and best friend, for life together in love and all the joys and blessings she brings, every day. Our sons and their families are also to be thanked for the blessings and joys they bring to us. We are thankful for and to Stephen and Caroline and their children, Maddie, Annie, Jack, and Ford; and Karl and Lauren. Great gratitude to God!

Jim has been blessed by an understanding wife, Doris, and daughter, Rachel, and congregation and is appreciative of all those who prayerfully encourage efforts to speak to a wider world beyond the narrow confines of a single parish.

Jim and Don are also grateful to our superb editor and friend, Robin Parry. Robin's insights, support, and kindnesses enhance all we do and we could not ask for a better editor and colleague in the field of publishing. For our friendships, we are deeply glad! We also wish to thank

Springer for allowing us permission to quote passages from Amos's brilliant volume on Martin Bucer.

This book is dedicated to the memory of a scholar and friend who did as much for Bucer studies as anyone. David F. Wright taught and was dean of the Faculty of Divinity in New College, the University of Edinburgh. David was a keen and judicious scholar who made Bucer accessible to English-speaking readers. He promoted the scholarly study of the Strasbourg reformer with great competence and grace. Scholars and students are deep in debt to David. We are honored to dedicate this book to his memory and in thanksgiving to God for his life.

One of David Wright's most distinguished students is Jon Balserak of the University of Bristol. Jon has graciously written the foreword to this book for which we are most appreciative. He is a very valued friend to both of us; and we are really delighted and honored that Jon helped us in this meaningful way!

Most of all, we offer this book on Martin Bucer in gratitude for Bucer's life and ministry and for his theological insights, which continue to nurture and guide us. Bucer believed "only the Christian life is a happy and blessed life." We find this to be so. We want to share the treasures of Christian belief and Christian life with our readers and all others. We confess, with Bucer, that Jesus Christ is "the fountain of life and every good gift, able to impart to us even his divine and eternal life as he has received it from the Father [John 5:26]." And we ask with Bucer: "Why should we not dedicate ourselves wholeheartedly to him and trust in him with an unwavering confidence that we shall be delivered by him from every evil and endowed with all good gifts, both temporal and eternal?"[6]

So we believe; and so we live.

6. Bucer, "Visitation of the Sick" in *Common Places*, 443–44.

INTRODUCTION

Welcome to Martin Bucer!

WE ARE PLEASED TO present this book as a "gateway to Bucer." We hope to present Martin Bucer's theological thought to those who are not—or only a "little"—acquainted with one of the great sixteenth-century Protestant reformers. Bucer was highly regarded by his contemporaries as a theologian of deep learning and genuine Christian piety. His theological insights were very important, especially to the more widely known and remembered theologian of Geneva, John Calvin (1509–64).

Martin Bucer (1491–1551) was a pastor in Strasbourg whose work helped establish the Reformed theological tradition in churches in Europe. He wrote voluminously, though not many of his writings are available today in English. Bucer was a key figure in trying to bring together differing viewpoints, particularly at the Colloquy of Marburg (1529), which Martin Luther and Huldrych Zwingli both attended. He participated in significant colloquies between Protestant and Roman Catholic theologians held at Worms and Regensburg. Bucer represented a "moderate Protestantism" in Europe and was always eager to seek ecumenical answers in a yeasty time of conflict and tensions among those who held differing confessions of faith.

We hope to show that while Bucer's work was important for the emerging Protestantism of his times, his insights are also significant in providing meaning and nurture for Christians today. We believe this Strasbourg reformer, who spent his last years in England when King Edward VI was trying to establish the English church, has vital things to say for twenty-first century Christian churches throughout the world. Bucer's convictions can help shape our own beliefs and give directions for churches and our Christian lives today.

We call this book a "gateway to Bucer." It is written to be an introduction and a "companion" to Bucer's life and thought. We have written for those who do not have extensive—or even any—specialized backgrounds in the study of Christian theology. We hope those with some familiarity with Christian thought—such as pastors, students, and lay persons in churches—will find this book helpful. If they are hearing of Bucer for the first time, we hope our presentation will be fresh and accessible. This book cannot cover the range of Martin Bucer's theological thought. It is not a "technical theological book." While we will examine topics that have engaged theologians in deep and detailed discussions in the past, we have tried to write as clearly and straightforwardly as we can. We want readers to hear Bucer's own voice. But we also try to explain the meanings and significance of what he wrote. We also want to convey key characteristics of his theology that can be important for us today.

Our book is structured according to theological topics after initially presenting a sketch of Bucer's life and work. We try to explore what each topic in Bucer meant for him . . . and for us. We point out places where Bucer's views differed from those of other Protestant reformers. Bucer did not proceed as "systematic theologians" do today in presenting detailed treatments of the various theological doctrines. But his theology emerges through his various works, including his biblical commentaries, where he directly engaged biblical texts. Bucer was an interpreter of Holy Scripture who wanted the church's theology to be grounded in the Word of God we encounter in the Bible.

As we point out below, Bucer believed "true theology is not theoretical or speculative, but active and practical. Indeed, the end of it is to act, that is to live a godly life." We resonate with this conviction and hope this book will instill a love of theology and also show theology's importance for helping us live faithful Christian lives. We believe Bucer's theology can energize those who seek a deeper Christian faith and provide a solid basis for living a dedicated life as a disciple of Jesus Christ in today's world.

1

MARTIN BUCER'S LIFE

At the 1529 Marburg Colloquy, where Luther and
Zwingli, Oecolampadius and Melanchthon, and Martin
Bucer met with others to hash out an agreement about the
Lord's Supper, Bucer asked Luther about his willingness to
discuss matters with him (Bucer). Luther replied "I am not
interested in what you teach in Strasbourg. I do not wish to
be your teacher. You have my writings and my confession."
When Bucer then asked whether Luther would even see
them as brethren, Luther said, rudely: "I am neither your
lord, nor your judge, nor your teacher. Your spirit and our
spirit do not agree with each other. It is obvious that we do
not have one and the same spirit. For it cannot be one and
the same spirit, when in one place the words of Christ are
simply believed, and in another place this belief is rejected,
contested, disavowed, and violated with all sorts of mali-
cious slander."[1]

Martin Luther was brash, gruff, unpleasant, and rude
to anyone and everyone he perceived to hold views different

1. Köhler, *Das Marburger Religionsgespräch*, 129.

from his own. Martin Bucer was his polar opposite. The two men could not have been more dissimilar. How Martin Bucer came to be in Marburg and how he came to be one of the leading figures of the Reformation and how he furthered the cause of the Reformed will be the subject of the pages to follow.

Martin Butzer (but commonly Bucer) was born on November 11, 1491 in Schlettstadt, Alsace. He died at the age of fifty-nine on February 28, 1551, in England. His fifty-nine years were filled with incredible achievements in the field of theology and his attempts to mediate all manner of theological disputes between various non-Catholic segments of Christianity (Protestant and Reformed) left an indelible mark on the sixteenth century and beyond. His impact is visible, like a crater on the moon, in Reformed theology and Anglican theology to the present day. So who was this man?

To understand Bucer, it is important to understand what he produced in terms of written texts. The broad range of things he wrote illustrate both his wide interests and his wide knowledge. His works, beginning in 1520 with his earliest work and spanning the next three decades, concluding in 1551, range from occasional pieces to confessions of faith to doctrinal treatments to catechisms to an elaborate exposition of marriage and the married life to documents from his last years in Strasbourg. The critical edition of his German writings, published from 1960 through 2015 spans eighteen large volumes.[2] His Latin works comprise seven large volumes.[3] A small sampling of his works shows immediately the breadth of his learning:

2. Bucer, *Deutsch Schriften*.

3. *Martini Buceri opera latina*.

- *An ein christlichen Rath un[d] Gemeyn der stadt Weissenburg Summary seiner Predigt daselbst gethan,*[4] 1523

- *Das ym selb niemant leben soll, sonder anderen,*[5] 1523

- *Grund und ursach auß gotlicher schrifft der neüwerungen, an dem nachtmal des herren,*[6] 1525

- *Epistola ad Ephesios,*[7] 1527

- *Bekandtnuß der vier Frey vn[d] Reichstätt, Straßburg, Costantz, Memmingen, vnd Lindaw, in deren sie Keys. Maiestat, vff dem Reichstag zu Augspurg, im xxx. Jar gehalten, ihres glaubens vnd fürhabens, der Religion halb, rechenschafft gethan haben,*[8] 1531

- *Ratschlag ob Christlicher Oberkait gebüren müge, das sye die Juden, vndter de[n] Christen zu wonen gedulden . . . ,*[9] 1539

- *Acta colloquii in comitiis imperii Ratisponae habiti: hoc est articuli de religione conciliati et non conciliati omnes, ut ab Imperatore ordinibus Imperii ad iudicandum et deliberandum propositi sunt,*[10] 1541

4. To the Christian Council and Community of the city of Weissenburg: A Summary of the Sermon Held There.

5. That No one Lives for Themselves, Rather Others.

6. The Foundation and Exposition of the Divine Scripture Regarding the Supper of the Lord.

7. The Letter to the Ephesians.

8. Confession of the Four Free Imperial Cities Strassburg, Constance, Memmingen, and Lindau to the Emperor for the Augsburg Reichstag held in the 30th Year, Setting Forth Their Faith and the Religion They Hold.

9. A Christian Response to the Magistrates Concerning the Jews and What Christians Owe Them.

10. Proceedings of the Conference Held in the Election of the Government of Ratisbone: This is the Articles on Religion That Were Accepted and Not Accepted, as They Were Proposed by the Emperor to the Princes of the Empire for Judgment and Deliberation.

- *Catechismus Ecclesiae Et Scholae Argentoratensis,*[11] 1544
- *Psalmi,*[12] 1547

And yet, the works he produced only tell a part of the story of the life of a man who, though now largely forgotten, wielded unimaginable influence during his earthly sojourn. It is to those details that we will now turn. But before we do it is important to mention the older biography of Bucer written by Hastings Eells, where he makes the following interesting points concerning his reason for writing the book:

> [I] wrote *Martin Bucer* to satisfy students of the Reformation who "have found his footprints not only in Germany but in Switzerland, France, England, and other countries as well." There, under "The contributions of Martin Bucer to the Reformation," Eells lists: Reformer of Strassburg, Conciliator of the Lutherans and Zwinglians on the Eucharist; Imperial Statesman; Protestant Partisan (after Regensburg, 1541) and Reformer of Cologne; and Contributor to the English Reformation.[13]

BUCER'S EARLY LIFE[14]

Born and raised in the town of Selestat on the Alsatian plain, Bucer's home town was known for its religious population and its cramped living space. His family history lies hidden

11. Catechism of the Church and School of Argentoratensis

12. Psalms

13. "Bucer Study since 1918," Thompson, *Church History.*

14. Much more on the life of Bucer can be found in Greschat, *Martin Bucer.* Equally helpful, and in some ways more so, is the biography of Bucer by Eells, *Martin Bucer.*

in the mists and little can be known of his grandparents or his parents. There are several Butzer's enrolled in the city lists but regrettably there is no certainty regarding which were his grandparents. Martin's father was a man named Claus, who seems to have made his living making wine casks and who, according to Greschat, went to great lengths to provide for his son Martin's education.[15]

Concerning Martin's mother, nothing is known of her. She never appears in Martin's works and he seems not to have talked about her. We can't even be sure of the date of his birth as no records exist. Since he was named after St. Martin it is presumed that he was born on that Saint's Day, November 11. Our best educated guess for the year of his birth is 1491. Bucer never mentioned either the day nor year of his birth.

Martin, in all likelihood, attended the Latin school in the city, but, once again, records of such are non existent. If he followed the normal pattern of the day, he probably began his schooling at around the age of six and left the school for university at around the age of fourteen or fifteen. By the end of his schooling he was skilled in Latin and familiar with philosophy. At this point in his life Martin had no inclinations to theological studies. His future was open. What he would do next would set the course of his life.

THE DOMINICAN MONASTERY

Bucer was sent to the Dominican monastery in Selestat by his family, and at their insistence. This decision, made for reasons unknown to us, but sensible for someone of Bucer's obvious academic gifts and economic difficulties, would determine his course of further study and his lifelong

15. Cf. Greschat, *Bucer*, 11ff.

engagement with theology. Bucer entered the monastery in 1507, at the age of sixteen.

As was then common, Martin served a year of probation in the order. That completed, he took the vows of a Dominican monk and entered the phase of his life that would last almost a decade and a half. Later, having abandoned the order and negating his oath, he would express regret for his decision to enter the monastery. But while in the order, Bucer took full advantage of the opportunities it presented for study.

As to the particulars of this period and the exact nature of his studies we know virtually nothing. We can assume that he followed the general course of the day and that he studied philosophy and was introduced to theology, though the curriculum was heavily weighted towards Aristotelian thought. Theology proper was pursued by study of select texts of the Bible and their interpretation in the *Sentences* of Peter Lombard. Bucer carried out these particular studies in Heidelberg and Mainz (at their respective monasteries). At the conclusion of his studies, in 1516, Bucer was ordained a priest, in Mainz.[16]

In 1517, the year of Luther's "95 theses," Bucer was living in Heidelberg and studying at the university there, pursuing a doctorate in theology. He, for reasons not exactly clear, never completed the degree, although he was later granted a doctorate in Cambridge when he began teaching there.

In 1518 a catalog of his library indicates that besides interests in theology Bucer was also studying poetry and rhetoric and history, and the works of Erasmus. In other words, he was opening himself to humanism and its influence. And that interest would eventually lead him to

16. Cf. Greschat, *Bucer*, 17.

associate with Luther's efforts of reform and cause him to leave the Dominican order.

BUCER'S HUMANISM

When Martin Luther arrived in Heidelberg in 1518, Martin Bucer went to the disputation to see for himself what Luther was suggesting. He left the disputation moved and delighted and indeed entranced by Luther's views. Though Luther's debate counterpart was a Dominican like Bucer, Bucer was not at all persuaded by his arguments.

Sometime between the end of 1518 and the beginning of 1519, Bucer received the degree "Bachelor of Biblical Studies." Thereafter as he lectured on theological and biblical and philosophical texts, a break with the traditions and ideas of his Dominican order began to appear and he drifted further into the orbit of Erasmus and Luther. His theology was becoming more and more aligned with the great humanist and the great reformer. His was not a "road to Damascus" conversion to Reformation but rather a gradual, even paced, steady departure from the "old faith" towards the new.

The decision to leave the Dominican order seems to have begun to be formulated in 1519, though Bucer had never loved the order, but the final break wasn't made until September 1520 when Bucer began the long and difficult process of seeking release. This was no easy decision. Vows had been made, they had to be taken with utmost seriousness. He must also manage to find a living. Connections to various important persons within the papal circle allowed Bucer to find release from his monastic vows finally on April 29, 1521.

THE LIFE OF A THEOLOGICAL MIGRANT

From this point on, Bucer would spend the remainder of his life traveling and settling for a time and traveling again, and all the while trying to bring various segments of the burgeoning "Reformation" together, both for the spread of the gospel and for the creation of a unified front against the Roman Catholic Church.

Bucer would, in this period, serve as a court chaplain for Count Frederick, a preacher in the town of Landstuhl, and then at Wissembourg, until finally he arrived at the city of Strasbourg, a town with which he will forever be associated. Before arriving there, the penniless, excommunicated, exiled priest had married Elizabeth in 1522. Their union produced several children, three of whom had died of the plague, as would their mother on November 16, 1541.

Elizabeth Bucer, like Katie Luther, had lived in a monastery. She had married Martin and by doing so violated her vows and so was stripped of her clerical office. Her new husband took up a post and preached with evangelical zeal, which resulted in their having to leave the city under the cover of darkness, and so they arrived in Strasbourg together. She was pregnant. Her husband needed work, but finding none he found himself having to move in, with his expectant wife, to his parent's house.

Martin wasn't able to find an official position at this time so he began giving lectures to students willing to pay for them right out of his house. This period of their lives together was filled with difficulty, and Elizabeth herself would undergo nearly a dozen pregnancies and deliveries, most ending in early deaths.

Martin Bucer, residing in the city of Strasbourg in May 1523, was desperate for work, and he went so far as to write Huldrych Zwingli in Zurich to see if a position there could be secured. It couldn't.[17] Finally, unofficially, he was able to secure an informal position as Matthew Zell's chaplain. It was sufficient to hold body and soul and family together and Bucer was able to commence his long and fruitful career as a theological writer.

STRASBOURG REFORM

Bucer's time in Strasbourg was marked by a widening rift with his former supporters and his hero Erasmus. In 1530 an anonymous booklet defending the Strasbourg reformers was published. Bucer was its author. Erasmus despised it and wrote a very abrasive response to it. Bucer read Erasmus' tractate in September of that same year and he let the response he wanted to publish die on the vine. But the rift was established and it would never be healed. Meanwhile Bucer occupied himself with writing and teaching and striving with all his might to bring about some measure of agreement between the Reformed and Protestant factions at the Diet of Augsburg.

But now he faced a two-front war. On one side were the Catholics and on the other, the Anabaptists, who disliked his position of leadership among reformers in Strasbourg and did their best to undermine him. Chief among them was Pilgrim Marpeck who had gained favor with the magistrates by providing a large amount of firewood during a shortage in 1528. Nonetheless, Bucer and his party were able to defeat Marpeck in debate and he was banished.

But Marpeck wasn't the only thorn in Bucer's side in Strasbourg. He also struggled against Sebastian Franck whose partisan *Church History*[18] riled the leadership of the

17. Cf. Greschat, *Bucer,* 55.

18. *A Universal Chronicle of the World's History from the Earliest Times to the Present: A "Church History"* (mid-1530s).

city and saw to his expulsion. These examples serve simply to show that Bucer was under constant pressure from all sides in Strasbourg and yet he was never robbed of his conciliatory and moderating positions.

CONCORD AND CONFESSION

Bucer's attempts to bring agreement to the Reformation, between Lutherans and Zwinglians, suffered a terrible setback in 1529 at the colloquy of Marburg. But all hopes seemed dashed in late 1531 when not only Zwingli, but the more moderate Oecolampadius both died: Zwingli at Kappel-am-Albis and Oecolampadius of the plague in Basel. 1532 was no better. Melanchthon was friendly enough, and even Luther, at the beginning of 1531, expressed a bit of charity towards Bucer, even writing on January 22

> I wish you would believe that, as I have told you at the Coburg I want to settle our discord even though I might have to live three times to accomplish it, because I have seen how necessary your fellowship is for us, and how the gospel was and still is disadvantaged [by our discord]. I have become so much aware of this that I am convinced that all the gates of hell, the whole papacy, all of Turkey, the whole world, all the flesh, and whatever evils there are could not have harmed the gospel at all, if we had only been of one mind. But what am I to do with something which cannot be accomplished? If you wish to be fair, then you will attribute the fact that I shun this unity not to stubbornness, but to the urging of my conscience and to the force of my faith. Since our discussion at the Coburg I have great hope, but this hope is not yet unwavering.[19]

19. Luther, *Works*, Vol. 50, Letter 238.

But conciliation was not to be. Not that Bucer stopped trying. He wrote, during this period, the *Confessio Tetrapolitana* [Tetrapolitan Confession], the *Wittenberger Konkordie* [Wittenberg Concord], and numerous catechisms. In 1533 The Strasbourg Synod met. Here, the aim was to crack down on the causers of chaos and disorder in the city of Strasbourg and ensure unity. And it was successful.

At the conclusion of the Synod, Bucer once more turned his attention to a solution of the disagreement concerning the Lord's Supper. To this end he composed his *Furbereytung zum Concilio* [Appeal to the Council] in August, 1533. Melanchthon loved it, but Musculus and Bullinger were extremely displeased with it. So, yet again, concord over the Supper proved elusive if not simply impossible.

Efforts continued nonetheless to bring together the Lutherans and the Reformed. Bucer and Melancthon were scheduled to meet at Cassel to hash out an agreement and Bucer hoped that Luther would also take part. He rallied the Reformed (the Zwinglians) and consulted with them so as to present their views accurately during the discussions. Scurrying around Germany, Bucer met with as many theologians as possible and finally with Melanchthon at Cassel. There, on December 30, 1534, Melanchthon and Bucer signed the *Cassel Formula*, which was essentially nothing more than a recapitulation of the Formula of Concord.[20]

When Bucer returned to Strasbourg, word had already reached the Swiss that Bucer had capitulated to the Lutherans and they would have no part in the agreement. Indeed, he so angered the heartiest Zwinglians that the wife of Thomas Blaurer started calling him "The Fanatic of

20. The Formula of Concord was composed in 1577 by Lutherans who wanted to stress that matters of theological indifference could not be made central issues. It then went on to describe the most important doctrines that all Lutherans were expected to hold, in "concord" (and hence the title).

Unity."[21] Bucer the concilitorian was becoming Bucer the betrayer so far as the Zwinglians were concerned. Consequently, their trust in him began to wane. Before long, it would be gone altogether. Bucer, sadly, failed in his efforts to bring the disputants together. All of his writing, all of his traveling, all of his pleading and encouraging simply fell on rocky ground and came, ultimately, to nothing. His many achievements and the impact he made notwithstanding.

Space limitations make it impossible here to go into the fascinating details of the many achievements of Bucer: his importance in matters related to France and its Reformed community; his part in the reorganization of the Hessian church; his influence at the conferences of Leipzig and Frankfurt and other professional activities. These must all take a back seat to the next major phase of Bucer's life and its most tragic, for things were soon to take a very sorrowful turn for Bucer.

THE YEARS OF SORROW

1541 was one of the most difficult years of Bucer's life. That was the year that plague arrived in Strasbourg and forced his colleague and dear friend John Calvin to an early departure back to Geneva. It was also the year that Bucer suffered incredible and unimaginable loss. As Eells remarks, "Bucer himself was not touched by the hand of death that snatched away his faithful comrade Capito, but his cup of misery was filled to overflowing when his wife and three of his children were stricken and died."[22] Additionally, Bucer's efforts at theological conciliation remained futile. At the Diet of Speier the Protestant party failed to carry the day and that

21. Cf. Eells, *Martin Bucer*, 179.
22. Eells, *Martin Bucer*, 308.

mainly because the princes and the cities simply could not come to terms with one another.

At the commencement of 1542, Bucer made the decision to marry the widow of his friend and colleague Capito. His reasons for doing so were simple: she needed a husband and he needed a wife to tend his home and two surviving children. Indeed, he did so with Capito's blessing since shortly before he died he asked Bucer to wed his widow. But the marriage also had its pitfalls. Many of Bucer's colleagues thought it was both a bit soon (his wife had not been in the ground even a year) and a bit inappropriate. After all, Ms. Capito had already been married twice before and her marriage to Bucer was her third. In spite of all objections, the marriage was contracted on April 21, 1542 and ceremonialized that same week.

The plague, meanwhile, had severely injured the effort of reform as it robbed Strasbourg of many of its leading lights. Capito and others were gone and the rest were beginning to show their age and infirmity. All of this made the burden on Bucer even heavier, even though he himself was now fairly old. But there was good news too.

> In this period when suitable teachers were rare, the Strasbourg reformer welcomed with particular joy an Italian refugee named Peter Martyr Vermigli, who came to the city in the middle of October, 1542. Peter Martyr was a master of Latin, Greek, and Hebrew, and he proved so satisfactory in the chair left vacant by Capito, that he was retained even after Fagius' arrival.[23]

Vermigli was to become, with the help of Bucer, one of the most important second-generation reformers in Southern Europe.

23. Eells, *Martin Bucer*, 319.

When 1542 drew to a close, the era of Bucer's greatest vigor and influence also began to wane. He would live only nine more years and during that time he would experience the disappointment of the failure of his grand program of harmony among the non-Catholics. Politically the winds were against him from the very beginning and the contentious Luther and stubborn Bullinger made his work virtually impossible. The irenic spirit of Melanchthon and Bucer simply could not hold the ground against the bulldozing of Luther and Bullinger. The lines were drawn in stone and the die was cast and the fracture was institutionalized in the various and separate Confessions of the Lutherans and the Hyper-Lutherans on the one hand and the Swiss and South Germans on the other.

The strife would prove to be too much and Bucer himself would be driven from Strasbourg only to find refuge in England where, for a brief time, his influence rebounded and his significance gained new life. It is to that final stage of Bucer's life that we turn next.

ENGLAND EXILE AND THE END

The reasons for Bucer's forced exodus from Strasbourg are many. Like Luther who fled to the Wartburg castle and Calvin who fled Geneva, Bucer too faced mounting opposition and personal peril. The only thing to do was flee.

Bucer had arrived in Strasbourg in 1523 and he departed, with no chance of ever returning, in 1549. It's difficult to conceive the massive amount of work he carried out during those relatively few years, and yet he managed it all. His departure to England made sense, however, because he was very popular there, for the time being anyway.

So on April 6, he left, secretly. When he arrived in Cambridge, he was graciously received by Cranmer, who speedily saw to it that he was assigned a teaching post at the university. He also saw to it that Bucer was granted a doctoral degree for his many writings. This degree was necessary to teach at Cambridge and Bucer thought that it was a bit bizarre, but he agreed to receive it.

But even in England, where political pressure was slight, theological pressure continued to exert itself and Bucer found it impossible to escape the various theological disputes that were raging in the island concerning the Supper (a perennial problem) and "vestments." Wherever he landed on those issues, Bucer would find disgruntled colleagues on the other side. It came to such a state that even the peace-loving Bullinger himself, when hearing of the death of Luther, remarked acidly "I would really begin to hope for something better, if Bucer also were called by the Lord."[24] Bullinger believe Bucer was actually a *hindrance* to peace rather than a promoter of it!

It is doubtful that Bucer ever learned of Bullinger's comment. What is certain is that in July 1549, just two years before his death, Bucer was stricken by an illness that cheered his enemies with the prospect of his imminent end. Eells remarks:

> The strange, damp climate was hard upon him, and the change from Strasbourg cabbage to English roast beef was more than his delicate digestion could bear. Worse than any of those things, which usually make life miserable for pilgrims in a foreign land, was the weariness that now began to take its toll for years of strenuous toil. He was worried, homesick, discouraged, and unhappy. Of friends he still had many, but of the joy of living he had little.[25]

24. Eells, *Martin Bucer*, 405.

25. Eells, *Martin Bucer*, 405.

This sad state would only worsen in the final months of Bucer's life. And his alienation from his former colleagues at Strasbourg made the burden of loneliness worse. Finally, he wrote them, lamenting:

> When I took leave of you, no one uttered a word in reply, the French pastor alone excepted. Yet I labored among you with all fidelity, and there are few of you to whom I have not endeavored also to make myself useful in my private capacity. If you knew what I have suffered since I left you, you would, I am sure, be moved with compassion for me.[26]

They were not.

England was good to Bucer, but Bucer was not satisfied with England. Growing wearier by the day and more and more disappointed with the Reformation there, Bucer wasted away. Finally, on February 22, 1551, Bucer finalized his will, expiring on March 1, 1551. His funeral was held at Cambridge with England's theological luminaries in attendance. His books were sold, his widow provided for, his story over. But not quite.

Four years after his death a new monarch with Catholic sympathies ascended the throne and Mary had Bucer's body dug up on February 6, 1555, and burned after a sham trial for "heresy." But the tides of history turn strangely and when Elizabeth ascended the throne she appointed a commission to restore the "true religion" to the land and Bucer was restored to full honor on July 22, 1560. Naturally, they could not bury his body, but they could erect a suitable monument to his memory, which they did, placing a brass plaque at the site of his original grave which reads:

26. Eells, *Martin Bucer*, 406.

FIGURE 1

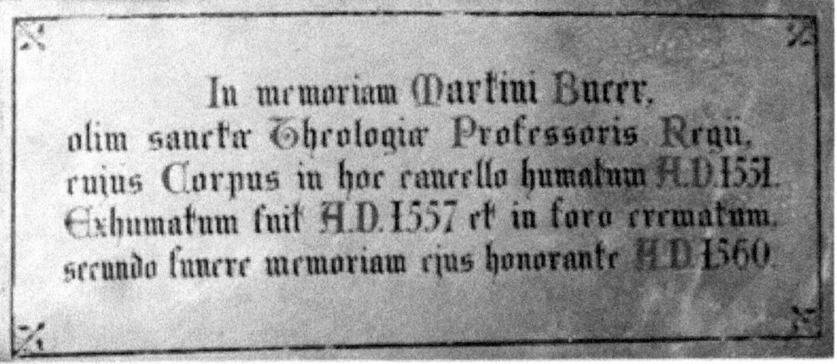

In memory of Martin Bucer, the Regius Professor of Theology.
His body was buried in this humble plot in 1551. He was
exhumed in 1557 and burned. And he then received a second
funeral honoring his memory in 1560.

This is a brief and concise memorial which fails completely to do justice to the man who did everything he humanly could to bring strong willed theologians together for the sake of the body of Christ. It is, and remains, a shame that at the end of the day Bucer was unsuccessful. Perhaps, then, the failure of his memorial plaque to do him justice mirrors his own failure to achieve his goal.

Yet, in spite of that failure, due more to the stubbornness or others than anything else, Bucer remains a fascinating subject. His theology is erudite and wise, and to the chief topics of that theology we now turn.

QUESTIONS FOR DISCUSSION

1. Why do you think that Bucer is largely forgotten among Reformed Christians?

2. What do you consider Bucer's greatest impact to be?

3. How do our experiences inform our lived faith?

4. Which of Bucer's writings do you think should be translated into English so it could be more widely known?

18

2

HOLY SCRIPTURE

The Bible was central for Martin Bucer. The Scriptures of the Old and New Testaments were the source of Christian belief and Christian living for Bucer. He was a person who was immersed in the biblical writings. Throughout his life as a pastor and professor, he lectured on biblical books and his lectures were turned into commentaries. These included Bucer's expositions of the Synoptic Gospels (1527), Ephesians (1527), the Gospel of John (1528), Zephaniah (1528), Psalms (1529), and Romans (1536; 1562). Bucer's biblical lectures became the basis for his teaching of theology, which he considered needed to be grounded in Scripture and is the way by which the Scriptures can be understood.

The Bible was foundational for Bucer as he developed his theological understandings. He also drew from the works of Martin Luther (1483–1546) and from the leading humanist of the times, Desiderius Erasmus (1466–1536). Luther was a towering figure of the Reformation era, with whom Bucer frequently interacted—in agreement and disagreement. A watchword of Luther's theology was what came to be called (in Latin) *sola Scriptura*—"Scripture alone." Holy Scripture alone is to be the authority for the Christian—more so than the church—and is to be the source or touchstone for all that Christians believe and how they are to live. The Bible, as God's inspired Word, presents Jesus Christ to people in an authoritative manner, one that can be depended upon.[1]

Erasmus was also a formative influence on Bucer. Erasmus and other Renaissance humanists advocated going "back to the sources" (Latin: *ad Fontes!*) to find the true sources of wisdom. For the church and its theology, this meant turning to the Bible and interpreting it. This is where the best theology is done. The Bible—and by extension the writings of the early church fathers—are the sources from which Christian theological understandings are to be developed. External church rituals are not as important as what Erasmus (and later Bucer) called "Christian philosophy" (Latin: *philosophia christiana*). This has been described as "a Christian way of life open to laypeople as well as clergymen, revolving around things quite simple and plain: following Christ in a life of piety, humility, peace, and love for one's fellow man."[2] What counted most, taught Erasmus, was simple faith in Christ and obeying God's commandments—which are aimed at the well-being of one's neighbors.

Bucer became committed to Erasmus' understandings which have been called "biblical humanism." This meant for Erasmus that a true theologian is

> first and foremost an exegete [interpreter] of the Bible, and that theology and exegesis [interpretation] were intimately connected. Consequently, he held that theology is best "done"

1. On Luther's understanding of the nature of Scripture, see Rogers and McKim, *The Authority*, 75–88.

2. Greschat, *Bucer*, 25.

> in an exegetical context. As to purpose, he maintained that theology should have a direct bearing on the Christian life: doctrine should be concerned with piety and right living, not with abstract questions.[3]

Bucer "shared Erasmus's convictions about the relationship of theology and exegesis. Likewise, Bucer shared the commitment to theology as a practical and not a speculative enterprise."[4] As Bucer put it in his commentary on John 14: "True theology is not theoretical or speculative, but active and practical. Indeed, the end of it is to act, that is to live a godly life."[5]

THE AUTHORITY OF SCRIPTURE

Theologically, Holy Scripture is the source for theology because Bucer believed Scripture was the written Word of God. He said the "first principle of theology" is "God has spoken."[6] Scripture is the foundation for Christian doctrine and the only rule and standard for the Christian's life. Bucer emphasized this basis for theology in his "A Brief Summary of Christian Doctrine" (1548) when he wrote: "We would have you uphold these Articles before God, testing them by his eternal word, which he has given us in his holy Scriptures and which alone is infallible."[7] For theological doctrines to be valid, they must be drawn from God's "holy Scriptures" which are the only basis for infallible beliefs—beliefs that are true and will not lead anyone astray. Scripture is the solid source for what Christians believe. Bucer

3. Amos, *Bucer, Ephesians*, 7.

4. Amos, *Bucer, Ephesians*, 7.

5. Cited in Amos, *Bucer, Ephesians*, 7.

6. Cited in Amos, *Bucer, Ephesians*, 106. Latin: *Deus dixit*.

7. Bucer, *Common Places*, 78.

agreed with the early church and Augustine that "the sacred Scriptures teach and reveal with fullness, comprehensiveness, and supreme certainty all that necessarily belongs to eternal salvation."[8] Succinctly, Bucer wrote: "All doctrine must be derived from Holy Scriptures. It is not permissible to add or subtract anything (Deut. 4:2 and 12:32)."[9]

This conviction was the first of his twenty-eight theological themes which, Bucer said, are "the content of our preaching." He wrote: "*The basis of all doctrine.* Concerning the things of God, nothing is to be taught unless it is either expressly set out in the Scriptures, or may be truly and certainly proved from the same (John 5.39, 46f; Luke 24:33f.; Rom. 15.4; 2 Tim. 3:14-17)."[10] This same emphasis was expressed in the Tetrapolitan Confession of 1530 which Bucer helped write. The Confession indicated that the churches subscribing to this Confession had "enjoined our preachers to teach from the pulpit nothing else than is either contained in the Holy Scriptures or hath sure ground therein."[11] Christian doctrine is based on the Bible so that preaching will be in accord with what God has revealed as divine truth in the Scriptures.

Bucer highlighted the importance of the church's preaching being based on Scripture in listing questions to be put to candidates for ordination in the church. One question the candidate would be asked was:

> Are you persuaded that the divine Scriptures contain the whole doctrine of eternal salvation, and are you determined to derive from them alone, and according to the confession

8. Bucer, *Common Places*, 222.

9. Bucer, *De Regno Christi*, 232.

10. Bucer, *Common Places*, 78.

11. "The Tetrapolitan Confession of 1530" in *Reformed Confessions*, 56.

of faith of our Church (which is the sum of the
doctrine delivered in the divine Scriptures, and
the catholic consensus of the Church of Christ),
everything you will teach the people committed
to you, and not to inflict upon it anything which
cannot be concluded and proved from them?[12]

The people of God must be led by pastors who believe
the Scriptures provide the way to eternal salvation and who
are committed to teaching what the Scriptures teach—and
nothing else.

Reference here was made to the "confession of faith
of our Church" and also to "the catholic consensus of the
Church of Christ." Bucer's commitment to the humanist
credo of "back to the sources," as well as the understandings
of the Christian church itself led him to help the church
recognize the value of the writings of the early church
theologians (patristics). These are helpful guides to Christian belief, their validity also being tested by the Scriptures
themselves. So, ordination candidates were also to be asked
whether they hold:

that any works produced subsequent to the ca-
nonical Scripture, of whatever content or origin,
must be tested by the faithful and measured by
the Scriptures themselves, and believed and accepted only if shown to be derived from the actual Scriptures: yet nevertheless that the writings
of the early saints and the orthodox Fathers are
to be received with respect, and the scriptural
and doctrinal expositions of later authors not to
be despised.[13]

All theological teachings—including those of the early
church theologians—are to be judged in relation to their

12. Bucer, *Common Places*, 274–75.

13. Bucer, *Common Places*, 260.

faithfulness to the teachings of Scripture. But orthodox writers of the early church have insights the church needs to hear, and their writings should be honored.

The authority of Scripture was a key element in emerging Protestant theology and in Bucer's theology. This raised an item of contention with the Roman Catholic Church. Bucer addressed this when he wrote: "Since faith rests on this primary truth as revealed by the Scriptures and the teaching of the Church, does Scripture's authority come from the Church or the Church's from Scripture?"[14] This was a question to be dealt with by all the Protestant reformers of the time since this basic issue of authority marked a sharp contrast between the reformers' view and that of the Roman Catholic Church. Bucer said Roman Catholics "endeavoured to make Scripture subject to the Church, by which they mean the pope." They sought, in other words, to curb the authority of Scripture. Their desire was that "the pope's rule should continue to extend as far and wide and be held as sacrosanct as it did when no one ventured even to contemplate the limit of the license enjoyed by churchmen." The Roman Catholic contention was that it was through the church that the Scriptures gained their authority since it is the church that recognizes Scripture and thus declares its nature and use. Said Bucer of the Roman Church: "They contend that the popes invest it with its status as the Scripture of God, and he who enacts a law is competent also to annul it."

To counter this, Bucer provided an illustration. He wrote:

> A prince sends his envoys on some mission with a brief setting out the business he requires them to transact, which is called their mandate. The point at issue here is whether the brief of the

14. See Bucer, *Common Places*, 184 for this discussion.

prince's commission acquires its authority from the envoys, or the envoys from the brief. Or to give perhaps a closer illustration: imagine a state which is wholly dependent on its prince who has promulgated laws regulating the conduct of all its private and public affairs. The question arises whether the authority of the laws prescribed by the prince derives from the state, or the authority of the state from the laws.[15]

Bucer indicated that

certainly all who teach or issue ordinances or make regulations in the Church are Christ's ministers and envoys, and must teach, ordain and regulate only as Christ has decreed. They have no power to act against the truth but only on behalf of the truth, and their entire authority has been given them for building up, not for destroying, the Church [see 2 Cor. 10:8; 13:8, 10]. They possess in the Scriptures a kind of brief of their commission from Christ. They possess also the Spirit (if they truly live up to their designation), to enable them to expound aright the contents of that brief. . . . The Church is subject to Christ the Lord, that in all things it should live according to his pleasure.[16]

As Paul put it, the "household of God," the church is "built upon the foundation of the apostles and prophets, with Christ Jesus himself as the cornerstone" (Eph 2:19–20). The Scriptures have authority because they convey the message of the gospel. The church *recognizes* Scripture's authority; but does not *convey authority upon* the Scripture. At the Colloquy of Regenburg (1541) Bucer sought to put

15. Bucer, *Common Places*, 184.
16. Bucer, *Common Places*, 184–85.

the issue more irenically, not calling to mind directly, the Roman Catholic viewpoint:

> It is agreed that all Scripture . . . is far greater than every human authority. . . . Hence it is futile and irreligious to question whether the Church's authority should be placed before the Scriptures, whether the Church can abolish or alter things handed down (*tradita*) in God's word, whether it can establish anything contrary to God's word. . . . But since no prophecy of Scripture . . . was produced by the prophet's own interpretation, for men of God spoke under the inspiration of the Holy Spirit [cf. 2 Pet. 1:20f.], God has also willed that the authority to interpret the Scriptures should belong to the Church, which is directed by his Spirit, so that the same Spirit who is the author of Scripture should also be its interpreter.[17]

The point for Bucer was that Scripture is greater than all other authorities, including that of the church. The Scriptures are inspired by God. The church interprets the Scripture under the direction of the Holy Spirit—who is "author" and "interpreter."

WORD AND SPIRIT

Inspiration

For Bucer, as for other Protestant reformers, God's Word and Spirit are inextricably bound up together. The Spirit's work in relation to the Bible is crucial. The Spirit, for Bucer, was the One who inspired biblical writers to convey what God wanted communicated in the Word of God, the Bible. The Spirit is also the interpreter of Scripture who brings the

17. Bucer, *Common Places*, 44.

message of God's Word into the church and into the hearts and lives of those who read the Scriptures. Inspiration and interpretation go together as the work of God's Holy Spirit.

Bucer saw the Spirit as the "author" of the Bible. By this, Bucer meant the Spirit inspired biblical writers. Their written message is the message of the Holy Spirit, what God wanted to convey through the human, biblical writers. God uses human writers, inspired by the Spirit, to be the means by which the Word of God is recorded and becomes the source of all Christian belief and practice.

Bucer used various expressions to convey this conviction. He spoke of the Scriptures as having been "written by the Holy Spirit," written at "the Spirit's command." The Spirit is the author of "the whole of Scripture."[18]

But Bucer also recognized the role played by the human writers of Scripture, especially in his biblical commentaries. Biblical writers, inspired by the Spirit, spoke the revelation of God—which is certain. Bucer never ventured into a discussion of the precise nature of biblical inspiration in relation to the writers of Scriptures. This is a divine mystery—God used humans, in all their varied thought forms and forms of expression (and in all the types of biblical literature) to speak the Word God wanted communicated through Scripture. There are transcription errors in Scripture in which the writer keeps to the sense rather than the exact words of a quotation; or, there are differences in the exact order of narratives with each other; or differences of times and person in certain biblical stories. But these very "human" dimensions do not detract from the ultimate conviction that it is from the Holy Spirit that the Scriptures originate and from whom Scripture gains its authority as God's written Word. The Bible is unique—and authoritative. Bucer noted that in no other book do we find

18. A most helpful study of Bucer is Stephens, *The Holy Spirit*.

the nourishment and enliving of the saints. This uniquely equips them to serve God because it is only in the Scriptures that we know of God's will and goodness, which leads them to true godliness.

The Scriptures are God's Word to the church and are thus authoritative for the church's belief and practice. Every decision of the church should be in accord with the teachings of Scripture. In the church, the elect of God will hear the voice of the Divine Shepherd, Jesus Christ. As Bucer put it in his commentary on Zephaniah, only in the Scriptures can the knowledge of God be sought and perceived.

Scripture is authoritative as the inspired Word of God. For Bucer, the Bible is the only certain Word of the Holy Spirit. Scripture stands over and against every human word—no matter from what source: philosopher, theologian, or church council. Scripture is authoritative because in the Bible, God's Holy Spirit has conveyed all that is necessary for human salvation. This message of salvation gives Scripture its unique and unparalleled authority.[19]

Interpretation

Through all his work, Bucer maintained the Holy Spirit was the supreme interpreter of Scripture. Human interpreters use the best resources available to help understand

19. Greschat asks: "How can one know that the Bible is the word of God and not human writ?" He quotes Bucer: "'The Spirit, the comforter, who guides us in all truth according to Christ's promise, it is he who tells me this." "For Bucer," wrote Greschat, "the Bible could and should claim unreserved authority, not because of a quality of supremacy attributed to it by man but as a result of the simple fact that it spoke to people and changed their hearts" (*Martin Bucer*, 62). Later, he noted: "Bucer never wavered in attributing a central role to the Holy Spirit and in affirming that Christians lived a renewed life as a consequence of the liberating effects of the Spirit" (101).

Scripture. The human work of interpretation is one to which Bucer devoted tremendous effort. But, ultimately, it is the Spirit who opens the eyes—in illumination—to convey the message of a biblical passage or verse. The Spirit can work beyond the human efforts, which must be made—but which give way to the Spirit's leading and guiding. As Bucer put it: "Therefore to the Scriptures, to the Scriptures, to the Scriptures, they are the rule and guiding principle, but the judge is the Holy Spirit."[20]

A key way that biblical interpretation can take place is by the principle that biblical interpreters should use Scripture to interpret Scripture. This is an aspect of the "clarity of Scripture." God, through the power of the Spirit, enables the message of Scripture to become known to biblical readers. As they use the interpretative tools at their disposal, such as interpreting obscure biblical passages in light of clearer biblical passages, Scripture's word can become known to interpreters. This has been the way God works through the Spirit for interpreters since the early days of the church. Bucer can be characterized as indicating his belief that "the consensus of the 'Old Churches' [*veterum Ecclesiarum*] was guided by the Holy Spirit, and served to confirm the proper interpretation in the minds of the faithful."[21]

Those who faithfully seek to interpret Scripture will find the Spirit's work will happen, even as the Spirit may bring to mind different scriptural texts to help interpret one that can seem puzzling. For ultimately, God wants all people to read the Bible: God has "commanded His sacred books, which are all contained in the Gospel, to be read by everyone."[22] Without the assurance that the Spirit aids in interpreting Scripture, there is no hope the message of

20. Cited in Amos, *Bucer, Ephesians,* 96 n.67.

21. Amos, *Bucer, Ephesians,* 97.

22. Cited in Amos, *Bucer, Ephesians,* 97.

salvation, which the Bible conveys, would be understood. If the Scriptures were too obscure, the message of Christ could not be real in peoples' lives.

The clarity of Scripture is grounded in the conjunction of Word and Spirit. The Word conveys God's revelation; and the Spirit interprets the Word. The Spirit's work in the heart of believers is crucial for the true message of Scripture to be understood. All persons must be "mentally enlightened by heavenly light, and given a new spirit, the Spirit of God, the Spirit of true wisdom."[23] The believer must seek the help of God's Spirit to open the Scriptures and guide interpretation. As Bucer said: "Let us, with all the saints, unceasingly pray [to receive] from the Heavenly Father, through our Lord Jesus Christ, [for] the Spirit of God's [children], the Spirit that searches out the deep things of God."[24]

The work of the Holy Spirit in inspiring Scripture and as the ground for the authority of Scripture does not entail that readers of Scripture will "automatically" understand its meaning. Along with the divine work of inspiration must come the human work of interpretation. Bucer recognized interpretation required hard and diligent study. But its purpose is to interpret the Word of God and to pursue "this worthy knowledge, the knowledge I say of salvation and eternal life."[25] This is the most important work possible so Scripture study should be sustained, and he counseled that "all the divine books must be read and re-read and meditated upon day and night."[26] Bucer advised in his commentary on Romans that Christians should pray that the same Spirit who inspired the apostles to write Scripture—for our sake—will enable the exposition of Scripture in the church

23. Cited in Amos, *Bucer, Ephesians,* 99.

24. Cited in Amos, *Bucer, Ephesians,* 100.

25. Cited in Amos, *Bucer, Ephesians,* 100.

26. Cited in Amos, *Bucer, Ephesians,* 101.

to serve the same purpose for which the Bible was given to us.

In his lectures to theological students, Bucer stressed the need for pastors and theologians to know Hebrew, the original languages of the Old Testament and Greek, the original language of the New Testament. Pious scholars gain insight to the meaning of biblical passages as they study the different types of biblical writings and see these in light of the aim of a particular passage in relation to the book of Scripture where it is found; and, overall, to the aim of the Scriptures themselves (Latin: *scopus*). There are passages in the Scriptures that are difficult to interpret. But Bucer saw these as encouraging believers to study even more diligently and to seek the assistance of the Holy Spirit. But while there are biblical passages whose meaning is elusive to the interpreter, Bucer was firm that the doctrines of salvation are clearly conveyed in the Scriptures, beyond any difficulties in interpreting particularly unclear passages.

More broadly, Bucer believed the Bible should be interpreted according to its natural, historical sense—or what a biblical writer or passage was intended to convey as it was written. Bucer rejected allegory (a hidden, spiritual meaning beyond the literal reading) as a major interpretive method. He believed allegory imported human ideas into the Scriptures as given by the Holy Spirit. Erasmus, whose insights were helpful to Bucer, used allegory as a method of biblical interpretation, especially for the Old Testament. But for Bucer, the fundamental sense of Scripture, the way in which we understand what God was saying and doing, is the historical.[27]

27. Amos points out that "Bucer's practice of interpretation was informed by the understanding that the text could—and often did—include figurative meanings as well (metaphor, analogy, simile, and so on), which were included within the literal sense by the author

As a whole, Scripture should be interpreted as presenting Jesus as Messiah, God's Son, and our Savior. From the Christian perspective of faith, the Old Testament foreshadows or points toward the coming of Christ in the New Testament. Christ interpreted the Old Testament in this way. Thus it can be said, for Bucer, that besides having a historical reference in Old Testament passages, there is also a Christological reference. The Scriptures, in short, are fulfilled in Christ and in the church.

Individual Christians, in the church, are to seek the Spirit's guidance to help in interpreting Scripture. Each Christian receives the Holy Spirit and can trust the Spirit to guide as the Scriptures are read and meditated upon by Christians. In this sense, over against the Roman Catholic view that the institution of the church was the authority to say how the Bible must be interpreted, Bucer held all believers must read and interpret Scripture so the Bible's message is personalized and believers can be open and obedient to the Spirit's guidance on Scripture's meaning.

This need for personal interpretation is especially important since the doctrines of salvation are revealed in Scripture. Some teachings of the Scriptures are not directly related to salvation or not required as necessary for salvation. In these "non-essential" matters, faithful Christians can differ with each other on biblical teachings. But ultimately, everything must be tested by the Word of God in Scripture—including what Bucer himself taught! He wrote: "You ought both to examine (everything) according to the Word of God, and to judge as accurately as possible."[28]

---

and were best studied by means of literary tools," *Bucer, Ephesians,* 119–20.

28. Cited in Amos, *Bucer, Ephesians,* 105.

LIVING THE SCRIPTURES

The interpretation of Scripture and the personalized appropriation of Scripture's message of salvation for each believer will (and must!) lead directly from "knowledge" to "practice." Doctrine and practice go together. For Bucer, the Bible's purpose is practical. As the New Testament says, "All scripture is inspired by God and is useful for teaching, for reproof, for correction, and for training in righteousness, so that everyone who belongs to God may be proficient, equipped for every good work" (2 Tim 3:16–17). So if one's life is not changed or amended from the hearing and reading of Scripture, we have missed reading it in the way we must do to receive salvation.

In this sense, Christians must not only *believe* the Scriptures—confessing Scripture's authority; we must also *live* the Scriptures—growing in the Christian life of love of God and love of others.

Bucer emphasized this need for the expression of Christian belief through Christian living throughout all his biblical commentaries. "Correct knowledge" about God is not an end in itself. Knowledge must lead to action and to godly living. In discussing Ephesians 1:4, Bucer wrote that the knowledge we receive in Scripture is given "so that we may daily be transformed into the likeness of God by renewing our lives according to God's Word, and may be holy and blameless in His sight, in love."[29] It is not enough to learn the teachings of Scripture in order to be able to explain them clearly and to teach others what the Bible communicates. The message of the Scriptures must penetrate into the lives of those who read so that, by the work of the Holy Spirit, we can grow into Christ. Hearing and teaching the truth is insufficient; one must *live* the truth. Paul

29. Cited in Amos, *Bucer, Ephesians*, 107.

expressed this when he said the purpose of God's choosing us in Christ is so we can be "holy and blameless before him in love" (Eph 1:4).

In summary: the Bible is the written Word of God. Scripture is authoritative for Christians, conveying what we are to believe and how we are to live. As Bucer said, the Scriptures communicate the "knowledge of God and of Christ. We confess and teach that from these Scriptures, by the aid of the Holy Spirit and a true faith, there is to be taught and learned a true and living knowledge of the eternal God."[30]

QUESTIONS FOR DISCUSSION

1. Why was it important for Bucer to affirm the authority of Scripture?

2. What is the significance of affirming that Scripture has both a "divine" and a "human author"?

3. In what ways does affirming the inspiration of Scripture make the Bible unique?

4. Why is it important to use all resources possible to help interpret Scripture?

30. Bucer, *Common Places*, 78.

3

GOD[1]

The Reformed doctrine of God has bequeathed to the church catholic a God who is truly Lord, a majestic sovereign who rides in the ancient heavens. He exercises his own good pleasure eternally, affirming and attesting and delighting in his own perfect goodness; and he turns toward his creatures in that perfect goodness to enact his justice and his mercy. Utterly self-sufficient, gloriously free, this God seals the covenant with creatures through the blood of his Son, and is content to dwell with them. He does not leave himself without witnesses, for the whole cosmos speaks his name. For this reason, the God whom the Reformed worship and adore, is in fullness and in truth, humanity's chief end, its glory and its delight forever.[2]

1. The material in this chapter is drawn in part from Bucer's treatment of God in the Tetrapolitan Confession, Bucer's most lucid treatment of the topic in Moeller, *Bucers Deutsche Schriften*. Philip Schaff's introduction to the Confession is available online here, https://ccel.org/ccel/schaff/hcc7/hcc7.ii.ix.v.html. Accessed Feb 7, 2022.

2. Sonderegger, *The Oxford Handbook of Reformed Theology*, 402.

THOSE LINES PERFECTLY SUMMARIZE the view of God held by Martin Bucer, for he held to a robust doctrine of God. It naturally goes without saying that Bucer's understanding of the Divine was the fountain from which every doctrine he held sprang. It is critical, then, to come to a better understanding of Bucer's view of God if we are to fully comprehend both his life and his work.

The previous chapter delved into Bucer's view of Scripture. Scripture informed every doctrine Bucer believed and taught and the scriptural vision of God was the foundation of his thought. Bucer was not a philosophical theologian (as that term is used today), he was a scriptural theologian.

THE 1537 CATECHISM

The chief sources of our investigation of Bucer's doctrine of God are the two short catechisms he published in 1537 and 1543 titled, conveniently, *Der kürtzer Catechismus* [The Short Catechisms].[3] These two editions represent the most mature stage of Bucer's theological development. Here he is at his most precise and most clear, primarily because these catechisms were composed for school children in Strasbourg. Thus, his language for children is the ideal means by which to explain his belief. The ability to explain God to children is rare. But Bucer has the gifts to do so.

The catechism follows the typical question and answer format. The instructor poses a very simple question and the child memorizes a very concise answer.

Beginning with the question, "Are you a Christian?," Bucer leads his intended audience to a deeper understanding of their faith. "How do you know you are a Christian?," he asks next and the child responds "Because I have been

3. Bucer, *Deutsch Schriften*. All translations are my own.

baptized in the name of the Father, the Son, and the Holy Spirit."

Working through such questions, Bucer arrives at the question concerning God. "What do you believe about God, Father, Son, and Holy Spirit?" the answer to which is a recitation of the Apostles' Creed. Which brings us to the first aspect of Bucer's thought: God is Trinity.

The Trinitarian God

The one God makes himself known as the Father, the Son, and the Holy Spirit. God is the triune God and there is no God but the triune God, who is not three gods but the one God.

Bucer does not attempt a philosophical explanation of this triune God, he simply accepts it as a fact, and a mystery. Each of the members of the Trinity in Bucer's theology will be discussed in the pages to follow, here the Father, and in the next two chapters the Son and the Holy Spirit.

In his catechism Bucer then asks the children who the members of the Trinity are and they respond "The Father, the Son, and the Holy Spirit." So Bucer narrows the focus of his catechetical questioning to probe the children's knowledge of God the Father. Who is this Father and what do we know of him?[4]

God, the Father

The Father is the creator. Bucer, as was true of all of his contemporaries, believed in the creative activity of God. The

---

4. The masculine pronoun is used throughout as it is the pronoun used by Bucer and his contemporaries. It may seem jarring and non-inclusive to readers today, but in Bucer's time it simply was the pronoun used.

world was no accident, it was a result of the direct, concrete, absolute intervention and action of God the Father. Were one to ask Bucer where the world and the stars and the moon and sun came from, he would perhaps express puzzlement and then respond "God, of course. Where else would they come from?" This creator God is all powerful and consequently the making of all things holds no difficulties for him.

Bucer then asks the key question, "What is it to believe in God?" And the children are to respond "That I can know God as God." Bucer then expands "Indeed, so you truly believe that God is your God and that he is the source of all good and does all things well so that he is the object of all your hope. What follows from this?" And the young ones respond "He is my Father." "And you also believe?" "That he is the Father of our Lord Jesus Christ, the first person of the God-head and that he is also my Father." "How is he your Father?" "In giving me his gifts and his inheritance." "What are God's gifts?" "All righteousness, piety, and love." "And what is his inheritance?" "Everlasting life."

The Father Who Gives

Bucer thus emphasizes in his theological overview of the God who is Father and creator that he is also the giver of the good things in life and thereafter. God the Father, then, is the God who gives. He gives himself in his gifts and he gives his Son as sacrifice. Key to Bucer's understanding of God is that he is the God who *gives* rather than the God who takes.

This contrasts with much of the theology of the Roman Church of the time when people were taught that God was there to receive from them. Their tithes and offerings and their prayers and their indulgence payments and their "sacrifices" through the Mass were all means by which God "received" from people. Rome took, in the name of and behalf of God. Adolf von Harnack makes this point when he writes:

> For this [i.e., the Roman hierarchy] party of Church politicians there was at bottom only one dogma—that the use and wont of the Roman Church was divine truth. The old dogma had only value and importance in so far as it was of a piece with the usages of the Roman Church.[5]

Bucer's vision of God, on the contrary, was of a God who gave. Indeed, the catechism continues "What do you mean when you say God is almighty?" "That God does everything for me through his power so that evil is defeated and all good given to me."

After delving further into the "creation out of nothing," Bucer moves to a discussion of the Second Article of the Creed, on Christ. Thus far the Catechism of 1537. What changes are there in the Catechism of 1543? It is, surprisingly, much shorter.

THE 1543 CATECHISM

After opening with the question "What do you confess concerning God the Father?" The answer, in contrast to the earlier catechism, is "Four things." And when asked to say what these four things are, the children respond "God is," "That he is Father," "That he is almighty," and "That he is the maker of all things."

In 1543 the question concerning the gifts of God is answered "Wisdom, piety, love, and all good things." And in connection with the question concerning God's creative

5. von Harnack, *History of Dogma*, vol. 7, 5.

purpose the answer is "That God has made me and all things out of nothing so that we might experience his goodness."

The catechisms thus share much in common though the second more briefly with minor changes to the substance of the answers. Therein we discover that Bucer's view of God is vibrant and focused on the goodness of God and the giving nature of the Father. God the Father, in Bucer's theology, is good, all the time.

Is this the perspective that we will find in the Tetrapolitan Confession? It is to that question that we now turn.

THE TETRAPOLITAN CONFESSION[6]

The Tetrapolitan Confession was the confession agreed upon by the four cities of Strasbourg, Constance, Memmingen, and Lindau. It was written by Bucer and others (though Bucer was the chief author) with the express purpose of informing Charles V of the beliefs of the Reformed for the Diet of Augsburg, 1530.

It begins with a plea to Charles to hear the views of the Reformed from the Reformed themselves. Chapter 1 is "On the Subject Matter of Sermons" and is a plea that the Reformed be allowed to preach their doctrine without interference, since it is orthodox and faithful to the Scriptures.

In chapter 2, the Trinity and incarnation of Christ are described so Charles can see for himself that they are teaching and preaching nothing but the truth. Bucer writes:

> Among these [he means the Reformed] is what
> the Church of Christ has hitherto believed
> concerning the Holy Trinity—viz. that God
> the Father, the Son and the Holy Ghost is one
> in substance, and admits no distinction other
> than of persons. Also that our Saviour Jesus

6. *Reformed Confessions*, Vol. 1, chapter 7.

Christ, being true God, became likewise true man, the two natures not being confounded, but so united in the same person that they shall never throughout all ages be sundered. Nor do they vary in these particulars in any respect from what the Church, taught out of the Holy Gospels, believes concerning our Saviour Jesus Christ, conceived of the Holy Ghost, then born of the Virgin Mary, and who at length, after he had performed the office of preaching the Gospel, having died on the cross and been buried, descended to hell, and was recalled the third day from the dead into immortal life: and when by various arguments he had proved this to witnesses hereunto appointed, was carried up to heaven to the right hand of his Father, whence we look for him as Judge of the quick and the dead.

This extensive quote nicely shows the tone and temper of the Confession and its clear purpose to show the Emperor that the Swiss reformers and their South German counterparts are no threat at all to either the church of Christ or the empire. Indeed, since the truth is found among them, those the Emperor should have his eyes on are the papists, who have swerved from the truth and no longer serve the Lord.

Chapter 3 of the Confession describes their view of justification and faith, chapter 4, good works, chapter 5, to whom good works are to be ascribed, and so on throughout the Confession the chief doctrines of the Reformed are delineated.

In the Confession, the image of God that is portrayed is the God known to the Emperor, and to all Christians, through the Scriptures. God is only fully knowable through Scripture and thus Scripture must set the tone for any understanding of God. Nothing in the Confession offers some new or revolutionary insight into the nature of God. It is the traditional view of God, traditionally presented. Bucer, in short, is a theological traditionalist in his doctrine of God in the Tetrapolitan Confession. But this is to be expected, since the Emperor would not like and would find distressing any wavering from what was known among Christians of God.

BUCER'S EXPOSITION OF PSALM 120[7]

Bucer was not only a theologian and statesman and calmer of raging spirits, he was an exegete. And his exegesis of Psalm 120 gives us an excellent insight into his understanding of God in a way that his theological and polemical works cannot. Written in 1546, and dedicated to the people of Bonn, Bucer here offers a lengthy exegesis of this psalm of praise.

Bucer's explanation of Psalm 120 is a line by line and phrase by phrase exegesis. He discusses the title and every line, in German, of the psalm in extraordinary detail. He sees the whole as a song of praise sung by the community of faith for the glory of God. This in spite of the heartache and sorrow that the human person is so subject to.

Psalm 120:

> A Song of Ascents. [1]In my distress I cried to the LORD, And He heard me. [2]Deliver my soul, O LORD, from lying lips And from a deceitful tongue. [3]What shall be given to you, Or what shall be done to you, You false tongue? [4]Sharp arrows of the warrior, With coals of the broom tree! [5]Woe is me, that I dwell in Meshech, That I dwell among the tents of Kedar! [6]My soul has dwelt too long With one who hates peace. [7]I am

7. Bucer, *Deutsch Schriften*, Bd 17, 17ff.

for peace; But when I speak, they are for war.
(Ps 120:1–7 NKJV)

Bucer observes of verse 1 that here we learn that God is trustworthy because he always hears and responds to our prayers. For Bucer, the trustworthiness of God should never be minimized. God can be trusted. God should be trusted. Because God has shown himself willing to hear the prayers even of those in distress. And this is an important point, since for many of Bucer's contemporaries any misery in life was seen to be the punishment of God for sins committed and thus praying for relief from such misery would be praying contrary to the will and purpose of God himself. The notion expressed by Bucer in his exposition of the psalm shows that for Bucer the mercy of God trumps the judgment of God. God wishes to extend mercy even to the wayward. They need but ask.

So complete is Bucer's exegesis that on verse 1 alone, in the critical edition, the commentary extends from page 27 to page 33. His exposition of verse 2 occupies pages 33 through 35 and he spends his time there making the point that God's good grace abides with believers through the accusations and misrepresentations of the false. God is true to his children even should every false tongue rise up to accuse them before him. God is faithful even if the Turk should conquer!

Verses 3–6 delve further into the attacks of the evil and God continues to exercise faithfulness to his children. "Poor man, what help is there for you when the false tongues strike and when God seems not to observe the cruelty, when you lie in the net and feel yourself about to be dragged down?" Fill your heart with faith and see the goodness of God come to your rescue! You may dwell in hardship, but wait on God's deliverance and you will experience his peace. That is how Bucer views these verses and he festoons his commentary with citations from other psalms in order to bolster his reader to faith and trust in the faithful and trustworthy God.

The conclusion of the psalm, verse 7, elicits this insightful point from Bucer:

> Every faithful person who, through our Lord Jesus Christ, has peace with God and knows that his sins are forgiven and that he will forever know God as his merciful father also wishes that every person might know this same Gospel and so preaches it to all so that all might have faith and the peace of Christ.

Bucer's God is the merciful God who wishes all to experience his mercy. Bucer's God is the kind God who wishes to pour his kindness on all who will receive it. Bucer's God is the loving Father who sends his beloved Son into our world so that lost and despairing people can find and know hope and peace.

Bucer concludes his exposition of Psalm 120 with these words: "So may eternal praise, honor, and glory be to God and may his people hold to him, learn of him, lead to him, trust in him through all their trials and sorrows and their war with the world and the Antichrist. Amen."

Amen! In our next chapter we will turn to a consideration of Bucer's Christology. A Christology, it's worth remarking, that is just as vibrant and just as moving as his doctrine of God.

QUESTIONS FOR DISCUSSION

1. Do you think Bucer's understanding of God is "orthodox"?

2. How do you see Bucer's view differing from yours?

3. Do you think that Bucer's view of God is similar to Luther's and Calvin's and Zwingli's?

4. How would you change Bucer's explanation of God?

4

JESUS CHRIST

Martin Bucer's Christology, like his theology (doctrine of God), is explicated most fully in his Catechisms. Two of these were referenced before, in the previous chapter. The other will be our primary source here in this discussion since it has the fullest Christological development.[1]

Presented in the question-and-answer style of catechisms, Bucer uses as his base text the Apostles' Creed. That Creed is worth citing here in full:

> I believe in God, the Father almighty, creator of heaven and earth. I believe in Jesus Christ, his only Son, our Lord, who was conceived by the Holy Spirit and born of the virgin Mary. He suffered under Pontius Pilate, was crucified, died, and was buried; he descended to hell. The third day he rose again from the dead. He ascended to heaven and is seated at the right hand of God the Father almighty. From there he will come to judge the living and the dead. I believe in the

---

1. 'Kurtze schrifftliche erklärung,' 1534, Bucers *Schriften*, Bd 6/3, 53ff.

> Holy Spirit, the holy Christian church, the communion of saints, the forgiveness of sins, the resurrection of the body, and the life everlasting. Amen.[2]

The first article of the Creed deals with God, the Father. The second with Jesus Christ, his Son. And the third, the Holy Spirit. Since the very early days of the Christian church it was normal for theology to follow this pattern and discuss, in order, the Father, the Son, and the Holy Spirit. Bucer follows that pattern unwaveringly.

Bucer is also unwavering in his orthodoxy regarding each of the statements made of Jesus. That is, Bucer asserted the literal truth of each aspect of the creedal statement. Jesus is God's only begotten Son. He is literally our Lord. He was literally conceived by an act of the Holy Spirit; he had no human father. He suffered under Pilate via crucifixion and he died. But he also, literally, rose from the dead. He ascended to heaven, bodily, literally, and sits even now at the right hand of the Father from whence he will literally return to earth to carry out God the Father's divine judgment on all. Bucer would not have doubted the absolute truth of each of those statements.

But Bucer was not willing simply to make a statement regarding Christ. Those statements, those truths, required explanation. It is one thing to say that Jesus was born of Mary, but Bucer wanted to describe, for believers, what it *meant* to Christians that Jesus was the Virgin's son. Bucer, in other words, wanted to address the "so what" of the Creed.

HOW IS JESUS GOD?

In his Q and A on the Second Article of the Creed, Bucer begins "Do you believe in only one God?" This is a sensible

2. Bucers *Schriften*, 6/3, 56.

question considering the fact that the student has been asked about their faith in God the Father and now about their faith in God the Son. How can one believe in One God if one believes that the Father is God and that the Son is God? Here, in short, the trinitarian question arises. How is Jesus God?

Asked if the student believes in only one God, the response given is "One God is also Father, Son and Holy Spirit." "But Jesus is the name of the Lord born as a man to Mary." "Yes," answers the student, "but he is also our mediator and redeemer through the Father. And that is what we ought to believe, as the Father leads us."

What Bucer is doing with these questions concerning Jesus is to affirm the truth of his deity and divinity without attempting to solve the trinitarian problem. How can we believe that there is only one God when we speak of Father, Son, and Spirit? The answer: we simply believe it because God leads us to believe it.

It is important to note that Bucer does not attempt a philosophical explanation of the trinitarian problem. Other theologians of the day were consumed by it, as they had been for centuries, but Bucer simply wishes to avoid philosophical debates and discuss instead the practical implications of the doctrine of Christ. How Jesus is God is of no interest to Bucer. He simply is, and that's what God wants us to believe. Who Jesus is as God is the topic that interests Bucer.

Jesus, the Mediator

"Why must you have a mediator with God," asks the questioner in the 1534 Catechism. And the answer: because God is not idle in righteousness nor in the punishment of unrighteousness. The mediator bridges the gap between unrighteous sinners and the righteous God. There are a number of scriptural texts that make this point and that the Catechist is expected to know. They include

- John 14:6. Jesus said to him, "I am the way, the truth, and the life. No one comes to the Father except through Me."

- John 3:16. "For God so loved the world that He gave His only begotten Son, that whoever believes in Him should not perish but have everlasting life."

- 1 Tim 2:5–6. "For there is one God and one Mediator between God and men, the Man Christ Jesus, who gave Himself a ransom for all, to be testified in due time."

- 1 John 2:1–2. "My little children, these things I write to you, so that you may not sin. And if anyone sins, we have an Advocate with the Father, Jesus Christ the righteous. And He Himself is the propitiation for our sins, and not for ours only but also for the whole world."

Augustus Toplady wrote that "Bucer's view of the sacrifice of Jesus was, importantly, that "Christ died restrictively for the elect only; but for them universally."[3] In other words, Christ's death brings salvation for God's elect. Jesus Christ died for the elect, not for every single individual. But every individual who truly confesses Jesus Christ as Lord and Savior by the work of the Holy Spirit in bringing

---

3. Zanchius and Toplady, *Absolute Predestination*, 81. The issue of the extent of atonement and salvation was part of the Synod of Dordt (1618–19). See Sinnema, "Doctrinal Dissension among Delegates at the Synod of Dordt," particularly "The Debate about the Extent of Christ's Redemption," 183–87.

faith—whenever and wherever they are (universally)—is one for whom Christ died and thus is one of God's elect.

Then asks the questioner "And what do you understand of the name Jesus?" The answer, very interestingly, is "Holy helper." Bucer here does not attempt to define the meaning of Jesus' name in either Hebrew or Greek or even Latin, but rather he defines the name by the function Jesus performs. Jesus is the one who helps us achieve holiness through his mediatorial act. He is the one who elevates us to the status of being the children of God and thus aids or helps us to be what he is himself and what God the Father made us to be. Jesus helps his children actualize their purpose and reason for being. Accordingly, it is not simply the Spirit who aids our holiness, as is often thought to be the case, but Jesus and even the Father, who is the "giver" of Jesus as Jesus is the "giver" of the Spirit.

The Catechism then provides even more details into the process of holiness by asking "Who does he help make holy?" And the response: the one who is sick and troubled and fallen in sin and trapped in its power.

"And what does the name Christ mean?" The answer: the one anointed as King. "Why?" Because he wages battle for us and through his power and through the might of the Holy Spirit he makes us to be victorious.

As the instruction of the Catechism continues it is made clear by Bucer that Jesus is the giver of all the things needed for salvation and for life even in the present. He is our Lord. And as Lord, he is capable of making us righteous and reigning and ruling in our lives just as he rules the world now and forever. Jesus, in sum, occupies a threefold office: as Prophet, Priest, and King.

THE THREEFOLD OFFICE

In 2013, in a genuinely fascinating article[4] on the topic of the threefold office in Reformed theology, Erik de Boer defines it as

> The concept of the threefold office of Jesus was developed in the explanation of the name Christ. The three distinct offices of king, priest and prophet in Israel are thought to be united in the one Messiah. Since the unity of all three offices in one person is not found in so many words in one specific text from the Bible, it is regarded as a theological concept. As such it was developed for the first time in the Heidelberg Catechism (HC). This article traces the development of the exposition of the Apostles' Creed in earlier Lutheran and reformed catechisms.

De Boer then cites this intriguing comment of Bucer:

> In those days kings, priests, and, prophets were anointed and thus inaugurated in their office. Yet Christ is the king of kings, the highest priest, and the head of the prophets, who does not rule by the external means of power, nor sacrifices stupid beasts, nor teaches and chastises only by means of his voice, but he rules the minds, the willing ones, unto salvation forever.

De Boer, citing Bucer again:

> Since therefore it was to this splendid realization that Jesus was destined by that divine anointing of the Holy Spirit, by right he had to be anointed for all God's children and by it be inaugurated in his reign, priesthood, and prophetical task (*munus*). And for this reason he is rightly called

---

4. De Boer, *Skriflig/In Luce Verbi* 47(2), Art. #682.

the Anointed, without any qualification, by *antonomasia*; it has the same bearing as if he would be called King.

And, finally, De Boer observes

There is no single text from the Bible where the three offices are singled out from the structures of the Old Testament and applied together to Christ. The figure of Melchizedek, the priest-king of Psalm 110, is a type of Christ, as explained in the Letter to the Hebrews. This Letter attributes the full realisation of the office of high priest to Christ. The attribution of the three offices to Christ was born from a systematic reflection on Scriptural passages.

De Boer is worth citing in this context so thoroughly because he says so well what must be said in this connection and he sets Bucer's own ideas in the wider context of the theological world of his day.

Martin Bucer is certain of the fact that Jesus is the mediator who simultaneously occupies three offices. He is the Prophet who speaks for God, the Priest who brings us into communion with God, and the King who rules our lives and the whole world. He is, in sum, God. But he is also man.

THE HUMANITY OF JESUS

Reformed theologians like Martin Bucer were utterly convinced that *finitum non capax infiniti* (the finite cannot comprehend the infinite). How, then, is it possible to talk about the finite human form of Jesus being (comprehending, in the sense of containing) the infinite God?

That question, like the trinitarian question, was posed not for philosophical reasons but for theological reasons. That Jesus is God is never disputed in Reformed theology, nor in Bucer. Rather, what that truth *means* was the focus for Bucer and other Reformed theologians.

Michael Allen states it very well:

> Along with belief that the Son remains human throughout eternity to come, Reformed churches have also insisted that Jesus took on full humanity such that every aspect of human existence characterizes the life of the incarnate Son. The only exception to this claim would be sin (which is not essential to humanity anyway); for Jesus did not succumb to temptations as all other humans do, and his own character was not marred by depravity.[5]

Martin Bucer would whole-heartedly agree with this view. He would also fully agree with the viewpoint expressed by John Owen, the Puritan Divine, when he wrote

> each nature operates in him according unto its essential properties. The divine nature knows all things, upholds all things, rules all things, acts by its presence everywhere; the human nature was born, yielded obedience, died, and rose again. But it is the same person, the same Christ, that acts all these things—the one nature being his no less than the other.[6]

Jesus, in the theology of Martin Bucer, and in the theology of his Reformed colleagues, was fully God and fully man, with no diminishment of either. How that can be is a mystery that only God can know. That it is, though, is simply the truth which Christians accept.

It is no mere speculative notion though, for if Jesus is not fully God, his sacrificial death is incapable of rendering

5. Allen, *Reformed Theology*, 66–67.

6. Allen, *Reformed Theology*, 69.

salvation because he is just another human being. And if he is not fully man, then his sacrificial death is no authentic sacrifice for sin. In this connection Allen observes

> The cross and its message of judgment upon evil marks the full measure of pain and wrath experienced by Jesus. Reformed theologians showed a willingness to reconceive a traditional doctrine, even a creedal doctrine, so as to affirm the depths of this abandonment to punishment.[7]

A further important aspect of the Christology of Martin Bucer is his view of Jesus as teacher. It is to that issue that we now turn our attention.

JESUS THE TEACHER

Bucer had a good deal to say about the teachings of Jesus. Aside from his theological works per se he also wrote exegetical volumes. Most notably, he wrote a commentary in 1527 on the Synoptic Gospels in which he naturally treats the Sermon on the Mount, the segment of the Gospel of Matthew where the teachings of Jesus are assembled into their largest continuous expanse.[8] This commentary is perhaps the best example of Bucer's understanding of Jesus the teacher.

A few examples will suffice to demonstrate the insight of Bucer on the teachings of Jesus and of Jesus the teacher. First of all, Jesus teaches his disciples to be good not for the sake of goodness itself but for the sake of the other, the neighbor. The so-called "golden rule" of Matthew 7:12 is the perfect example of this teaching. "Do unto others what you would have others do to you," said Jesus. For Bucer, this

7. Allen, *Reformed Theology*, 67.

8. On this commentary, see the very helpful dissertation (unpublished) of Tait, *A Method for the Christian Life.*

means that life is lived reciprocally. Believers, disciples, live their lives in tandem with others, joining with them in their struggles and their joys and in sum by doing so they imitate God who joins them in their struggles and in their joys.

Love your neighbor, Bucer asserts. Tait remarks in this connection:

> The "neighbor," in Bucer's view, is anyone with whom we are brought into contact, whether by blood relationship, physical proximity, association in work or some other activity, or simply by a chance meeting, as when the Samaritan found a stranger bleeding by the side of the road. The quality of being a neighbor is thus largely independent of our choice or inclination.[9]

But for Bucer the Christian life is not simply summarized in the love commandment. It is multifaceted. The Christian life is also expressed in self-denial. And self-denial is the chief aim of the first four of the Beatitudes, according to Bucer. Or, in his own words, in these Beatitudes Jesus "wanted to encourage self-denial, the mortification of the flesh and of the world—namely that one should say farewell to the things that are present and receive from the Lord heavenly things."[10] Accordingly, in Bucer's Christology, adhering to the teaching of Jesus supplies believers with the tools they need to transition from a life in this world to life in the next.

But having an eye to the next life is itself not the sum and substance of Christian self-denial. Rather, the other side of the coin, as it were, is the purpose of self-denial in the present and for the life lived in this evil world. So Bucer explains "Christ taught . . . what should be suffered and

9. Tait, *A Method*, 228.

10. Tait, *A Method*, 314.

given up, namely everything, so that naked of all things we may offer ourselves to him to be made happy."[11]

Christ's teaching, then, aims to draw people into his sphere of love so that by love and in love and through love they might be fitted with the necessary tools of love and self-sacrifice so they might live in the present as the recipients of his good gifts and in the future they might live as the blessed and redeemed children of God in the presence of God for eternity.

CHRIST IN THE FIRST HELVETIC CONFESSION

The First Helvetic Confession was composed primarily by Heinrich Bullinger but Martin Bucer also helped write and refine it. Accordingly, we find in this important document, Bucer's solidified, matured Christology. The document was published in 1536 and stood as the statement of the Swiss Church's beliefs until the enlarged Second Helvetic Confession appeared in 1566. Philip Schaff notes

> The Helvetic Confession is the first Reformed Creed of national authority. It consists of twenty-seven articles, is fuller than the first Confession of Basle, but not so full as the second Helvetic Confession, by which it was afterwards superseded. The doctrine of the sacraments and of the Lord's Supper is essentially Zwinglian, yet emphasizes the significance of the sacramental signs and the real spiritual presence of Christ, who gives his body and blood—that is, himself—to believers, so that he more and more lives in them and they in him.[12]

11. Tait, *A Method*, 314.

12. Schaff, *Creeds of Christendom*, available online here https:// ccel.org/ccel/schaff/creeds1/creeds1.ix.ii.iv.html and accessed February 24, 2022.

The Confession is a series of brief statements summarizing Reformed faith, beginning with the Scripture and moving on to the interpretation of Scripture before it describes Reformed belief in God. Importantly, the trinitarian God is described without, at this point, any particularities of the Godhead enunciated. The Confession then takes up the doctrines of humanity and sin.

The article with which we are concerned here, however, is the eleventh. It is the longest to this point and in six dense paragraphs. The dual nature of Jesus and his full humanity are highlighted. He is, in the duality of his being though he is a singular being, the bringer of the gift of everlasting life and it is through him that salvation is granted. This same Jesus will, at the end of time, come to earth and judge those who are alive and those who are dead. He who is our "Mediator, justifier, offering, High Priest, Lord, and King" is also the object of our full belief and is the only source of all these gifts of God.

Bucer, Bullinger, and Jud with the rest of the theologians who wrote this amazing Confession were, in it, Christocentric. Christ is all in all. Indeed, the Second Helvetic Confession is the best commentary on the First, and on this point it does an excellent job of describing Jesus and what the authors of the First wished to say:

> Wherefore we do plainly and openly profess and preach, that Jesus Christ is the only Redeemer and Saviour of the world, the King and High Priest, the true and looked-for Messiah, that holy and blessed one (I say) whom all the shadows of the law, and the prophecies of the prophets, did prefigure and promise; and that God did supply and send him unto us, so that now we are not to look for any other. And now there remains nothing, but that we all should give all glory to him, believe in him, and rest in him only, contemning

and rejecting all other aids of our life. For they are fallen from the grace of God, and make Christ of no value unto themselves, whosoever they be that seek salvation in any other things besides Christ alone (Gal. 5:4).[13]

Perhaps that is the best way to conclude our present investigation. There "remains nothing, but that we all should give all glory to him, believe in him, and rest in him only, contemning and rejecting all other aids of our life."

QUESTIONS FOR DISCUSSION

1. Jesus is both God and man. How do you interpret that?

2. How does Bucer's understanding of Jesus align with your own?

3. How does Bucer's understanding of Jesus differ from yours?

4. If you had to summarize Bucer's view of Jesus in one sentence, what would you say?

13. Schaff, *Creeds of Christendom*, Vol. 3, 854.

5

HOLY SPIRIT

MARTIN BUCER HAD A vigorous doctrine of the Holy Spirit. That is, he saw the Holy Spirit of God to be active in many dimensions of God's work in the world and in the church. Though he did not give specific theological attention to the Spirit in a systematic way, it is clear he considered the Spirit to be deeply important to Christian theology and the Christian doctrine that constitutes the faith of the Christian church.[1] Bucer saw the Spirit's work as consistent with the New Testament portrayal of the Spirit who is at work—but not in ways that turns attention to the Spirit. The Spirit witnesses or points to Jesus Christ and establishes faith. The Spirit is active in the life of the church and in the lives of Christian believers. This ongoing work of the Holy Spirit means the Spirit's many activities are important aspects of Christian belief and Christian living.

1. David Steinitz wrote that "a dominant motif" in Bucer's theology "throughout his life" was "the cruciality of the work of the Spirit." See Steinmetz, *Reformers in the Wings*, 123.

THE PERSON OF THE HOLY SPIRIT

Bucer believed and upheld the orthodox teaching of the early Christian theologians and confessions of faith that the Holy Spirit is fully a member of the Godhead: Father, Son, and Holy Spirit. The Trinity is basic to Christian theology. Bucer presented this in the Tetrapolitan Confession which said what "the Church of Christ has hitherto believed concerning the Holy Trinity—viz. that God the Father, the Son and the Holy Ghost is one in substance, and admits no distinction other than of persons."[2] The three members of the Trinity are fully and equally God, sharing the same "substance"; but are together one God in three persons. This is basic for the church's theology and was Bucer's bedrock belief.

Most basically, the Holy Spirit helps the message of God's revelation in the Holy Scriptures to be known and understood. Bucer wrote that "we confess and teach that from these Scriptures, by the aid of the Holy Spirit and a true faith, there is to be taught and learned a true and living knowledge of the eternal God, of the unity of his divine substance, and the Trinity of the Persons."[3] The Spirit brings faith and from the Scriptures a "true and living knowledge" of God is conveyed. That knowledge of God includes recognizing who God is: one God in substance who is a trinity of persons. It is by the work of the Spirit that we come to believe that this is who God is.

From our understanding of who the Holy Spirit is, Bucer goes on throughout his theology to indicate what the Spirit does. The many pervasive and important activities of the Spirit led a German theologian, August Lang, in 1900 to say that Bucer's whole theology can be called "a theology of

2. Cochrane, *Reformed Confessions*, 56.
3. Bucer, *Common Places*, 78.

the Spirit."[4] Bucer's understanding of the work of the Holy Spirit can be seen in relation to the Holy Spirit and salvation, the Holy Spirit and the church, and the Holy Spirit and the Christian life.

THE HOLY SPIRIT AND SALVATION

The Bible is a book about salvation. For Bucer, the Bible is where the Holy Spirit speaks clearly. The prophets "under the impulse of God's Spirit and later apostles moved by the same Spirit were commissioned and sent to us as interpreters of the divine will. . . . They themselves gave us writing."[5] "Christ our Lord," said Bucer, "sends us to the Scriptures in John 5 and to the Holy Spirit the interpreter of the Scriptures."[6] We are to seek to understand what the Spirit is teaching us through Scripture.

In trying to understand Scripture, Bucer advocated seeking the guidance of the Spirit even as human interpreters use the tools and resources God gives to pursue God's message for their lives. The Spirit enables us "to expound aright" the contents of Scripture.[7] The Spirit is a gift to the church. For "all cogniscance of the word proceeds from the Spirit of Christ and the Church then was strongly endowed with this Spirit."[8]

Theologically, Bucer believed the Holy Spirit has revealed God's love in Scriptures so our salvation rests on God's gracious, electing choice of those who receive the gift

---

4. Lang, *Der Evangelienkommentar Martin Butzers*, 120. The phrase is: "Theologie des Geistes." A modern study is Stephens, *The Holy Spirit* where he explores the Holy Spirit as a "pivotal doctrine," 1.

5. Bucer, *Common Places*, 187.

6. Bucer, *Common Places*, 219.

7. Bucer, *Common Places*, 185.

8. Bucer, *Common Places*, 188.

of faith for salvation. Bucer said: "Let us also consider the eloquence and excellence of the Holy Spirit who infinitely surpasses all the Fathers for all their strong points. So lucidly and clearly does the Holy Spirit himself ascribe our whole salvation to the goodness and love of God through Christ, without, however, intending us to be completely inactive but to work it out, both in ourselves and among our fellows, according to the measure of the grace of God in us."[9]

God's grace in us, which enables us to accept the gospel message of Scripture by the work of the Holy Spirit, is the grace that gives faith in Jesus Christ. God enlightens human hearts "by his Spirit that they might recognise God's word addressing them."[10] Bucer wrote: "It is established that our salvation and eternal life are based on faith alone, faith in Jesus Christ our Mediator who by his death has so effectively caused the Father to be reconciled towards us that he treats us as sons and heirs and will bless us eternally."[11] Faith is the means by which the death of Christ to reconcile us with God becomes known and real for us. In faith, "we believe that Christ alone has reconciled us to the Father by his death, so that now we are his sons and heirs, and indeed joint-heirs with Christ. As a result of this the Spirit of sons [children] has also been given to us as an utterly reliable pledge of this inheritance, the Spirit through whom we cry with full confidence to God, "Abba, Father."[12] Without the work of the Holy Spirit, humans remain "dead through trespasses and sins" (Eph 2:15; Col 2:13). Only the Spirit can make one "alive to God in Christ Jesus" (Rom 6:11). Reconciliation, forgiveness of sin, justification, and new life

9. Bucer, *Common Places*, 112.

10. Bucer, *Common Places*, 174.

11. Bucer, *Common Places*, 320.

12. Bucer, *Common Places*, 319. Cf. Rom 5:10; 8:17; 2 Cor 5:18ff.; Rom 8:15; Gal 4:6.

in Jesus Christ are the results of faith in Jesus Christ given by the Holy Spirit. We are saved by faith!

Faith is not of human origin. Faith is the work of God's Spirit. Bucer said we speak of "the faith we have in the words of God and under the influence of the Holy Spirit."[13] Bucer always emphasized this initiating and sustaining work of the Spirit when he described or defined faith. He wrote:

> We have already propounded a definition of faith, giving as its meaning what Paul understands by the word whenever he affirms that we are justified and saved by faith. Everywhere he ascribes to faith freedom of access to God, confidence in invoking divine succour, peace of conscience and joy, and all of them through the Holy Spirit and by keeping closely in mind the merit of Christ. Therefore, he is bound to have understood by the term "faith" an unwavering persuasion of God's mercy and fatherly kindness towards us, created through the Holy Spirit and resting on the accepted sacrifice of Christ.[14]

In the gift of faith by the Holy Spirit, the promises of the gospel in Jesus Christ are assented to "under the guidance of the same Spirit."[15] In the gospel of Christ, God promises "his good-will towards us," along with "commands and exhortations to holiness of life." The gospel is taught, in which

> God sets before us what he has bestowed on us, and will henceforth bestow, through our Lord Jesus Christ, for we can attain the knowledge of God only by the knowledge of what he is and purposes to be to us. Therefore, through the

13. Bucer, *Common Places*, 192.

14. Bucer, *Common Places*, 172.

15. Bucer, *Common Places*, 176.

gospel is present this promise of his kindness in Christ our Lord, that through him he means to be all things to us, to forgive our sins and make us partakers of eternal life. Assent is given to this promise by those upon whom he breathes by his Spirit; by the Spirit alone can it be acknowledged as the promise of God. This assent is the evangelical faith of which Paul speaks [1 Cor. 2:5].[16]

For Bucer, the work of the Holy Spirit in salvation—through establishing faith—is the outworking of God's eternal predestination, God's election—God choosing those to be saved. The Spirit enacts God's election in those who become believers by giving the gift of faith. In his commentary on Romans, Bucer says that it is the Holy Spirit who is the "pledge" and also the "seal" of our election by God.[17]

As the different dimensions of salvation—sometimes called an "order of salvation"—unfold, the work of the Holy Spirit continues to be a major emphasis for Bucer. The Spirit binds all aspects of salvation together. God's election or predestination is followed by God's adopting or calling (vocation) those who are God's elect and will be saved. These will live a holy life and carry out the duties of love through good works (sanctification). Finally, in glorification, the saints live eternally to the praise of the triune God.[18]

In election, Bucer said that God's election to eternal life means God will also *call* that person—in God's time—and by the Holy Spirit will enable that person to believe God's Word. Bucer maintained election implies that a new

16. Bucer, *Common Places*, 176–77.

17. Correlatively, for Bucer, the "sin against the Holy Spirit" is a sure sign that one is reprobate—not elect and thus not a recipient of salvation.

18. On election and predestination and these aspects of salvation see chapter 6 below on "Sin and Salvation."

life in a believer will emerge that will be lived in conformity with the image of Jesus Christ in a person. This is God's purpose in election; and this is why God gives the Holy Spirit. The Spirit enables the elect to live to God's glory. The work of the Holy Spirit, said Bucer, is one of vivification—"making alive" the elect. The Spirit persuades those who are called by God to believe. This is totally the work of the Spirit. God's purpose in election is that the elect will know God, love God, and worship God as they live lives that are pleasing to the Lord. This means there is no merit within our selves that we might believe and come to faith in Jesus Christ. Our salvation comes from God through Christ by the Holy Spirit.

Bucer had a christological view of election. He maintained that God has elected us through Christ "before the foundation of the world" (Eph 1:4), meaning there is no human "merit," there is only the merit of the blood of Christ through which salvation comes (Eph. 1:7; 2:13).

In vocation (calling), salvation "begins" for those who are called and given the gift of faith by the Holy Spirit. This is a vocation to salvation. The Spirit illuminates those who are elected and called. The Holy Spirit is, said Bucer, the power through which our minds are "illumined" and able to receive the things of God and, indeed, desire those things. This goes directly against our natural, sinful nature. The Spirit works this illumination through the Word of God, in Scripture and in preaching as the message of the gospel of the work of Christ is proclaimed. All this is the work of God's Spirit in salvation.

THE HOLY SPIRIT AND THE CHURCH

For Martin Bucer, the Christian church is a fellowship of believing Christians created by the Holy Spirit. When faith is established by the work of the Spirit's illumination and a person confesses Jesus Christ as Lord and Savior, the Spirit draws the new believer into the fellowship of other believers, the "body of Christ" (1 Cor 12:27), the church. There is an inward "baptism" by the Holy Spirit when faith is confessed and believers are drawn together in a corporate body, the church. The church makes visible, through Word and Spirit, the active presence of Christ in the world. The church is "a fellowship gathered by the Spirit of Christ."[19]

The church—as also individual Christians—live in constant dependence on the Holy Spirit. The Spirit leads and guides the church and believers. Neither the church nor Christians themselves can live independently of the Spirit's presence and help. They cannot build their own lives or achieve a righteousness based on their own abilities or actions. Christians in the church seek God's will and purposes for the life of the church and their own lives. They cooperate with the Spirit. Bucer wrote in his commentary on Romans that while the Spirit alone brings salvation, God uses our own energies so we are instruments for God as we live our lives for God. The Spirit works within the church and in the lives of believers to lead us into the lives God wants us to live.

The Spirit distributes gifts to the elect to be used for the upbuilding of the church and to meet the needs of others. Bucer wrote no one person receives all God's gift. God desires we should always have need of others and that we help one another. All gifts are needed for the ministry of the church. Each person in the church has need of the gifts of others. We all need each other. The gifts of the Holy Spirit are meant to be shared within the fellowship of the church and beyond, for the needs of neighbors and the world itself. While there are "varieties of gifts," it is "the same Spirit"

19. Bucer, *Common Places*, 206.

who gives them; and there are "varieties of service" and "activities" (1 Cor 12:4–6). With all these gifts, it is the Spirit who bestows them. Gifts are given for the upbuilding of the church and "the common good" (1 Cor 12:7), especially for unity and love, as Bucer indicated in his commentary on Ephesians. It is "the same Spirit, who allots to each one individually just as the Spirit chooses" (1 Cor 12:11).

Within the church, some may have gifts that can be used specifically as pastors and church leaders. Since preaching is a function of the church and since through preaching the Spirit works to bring faith, it was important for the church to be conscientious and perceptive in regard to choosing those who lead the church in its ministries, including the ministries of Word and Sacrament. Bucer advised that the church should always see and seek those who are endowed with God Spirit and who can build up the church. These persons should be recognized without regard to who they are or what their circumstances may be. This is a general indication of the Spirit's work within them and that they should be chosen for this ministry. The church does not need to wait for any special or "miraculous" signs. The church can follow this general indication of the Spirit of God.

The church and Christians who are members of the body of Christ seek God's guidance and direction for their lives and ministries.

THE HOLY SPIRIT AND THE CHRISTIAN LIFE

Serving Others

The continuing guidance of the Holy Spirit within the church and within individual Christians leads to the performance of service to God through good works, established and prompted by the Spirit. Bucer believed good works are

God's gifts and are fruits of the Spirit (Rom 8:23) in those who are saved or justified by God's grace. These good works follow upon one's justification or salvation and are not part of justification itself. The good works or fruits of the Spirit are works of God's pure grace and are done for the love of Christ and the sake of Christ. Like other Protestants, Bucer saw justification or salvation as God's work in giving faith by the Holy Spirit. Those who are justified live out their salvation by doing "good works," those expressions of faith which are God's will for how believers serve God. The "fruits of the Holy Spirit" in good works follow from justification, they are never the cause of justification. Good works express the work of the Holy Spirit in each Christian believer.

Bucer also wrote that "those who hear Christ and the Holy Spirit are eager to undertake and perform all good deeds in that order and manner which they acknowledge to have been determined for them by the Lord and the Holy Spirit."[20] The Spirit leads believers into the good works of service through which they grow in faith (sanctification) and express their faith. Particularly, the Spirit leads believers in the church to be concerned with "the care for the poor and needy. For the Lord expressly forbids his people to allow anyone among them to be in need (Deut. 15:4)."[21] Physical and spiritual needs are of special care for believers in relation to others. August Lang said that for Bucer:

> Christ works in each elect individual, and each individual, with his special gift, is an instrument of the Holy Spirit. Thus, through Christ's Word and Spirit, there arises the care of souls and the disciplined fellowship in which each member recognises it as his special task not only to see

20. Bucer, *De Regno Christi*, 257.
21. Bucer, *De Regno Christi*, 256.

> to his own growth in grace, but also to the salvation and edification of his neighbour's soul.[22]

All this is from the work of faith in Jesus Christ, established in believers by God's Holy Spirit. For Bucer, we become the children of God and are assured by God's Spirit that we are God's children. In this sense, we recognize and call on God as our "Father" while also recognizing all people as our sisters and brothers. We serve them. This is pleasing to God who created us to serve others, as the law and the prophets indicate. We are led into this service by faith. Only faith can detach us from ourselves and lead us into committing ourselves to God as God's children.

Prayer

A primary way the Holy Spirit is active in the lives of Christians is through prayer. Bucer did not set the practice of prayer as a way of discerning and understanding the will of God against the Bible. It is not as if one should choose either to read the Bible to find God's will for one's life or to pray to find God's will. Both go together for Bucer. For prayer is necessary as believers read Scripture. God's will in the Bible is not recognized and understood apart from the Spirit of God who gives us understanding of it. Word and Spirit are inextricably bound up together. Through prayer, which is our mind being elevated to God and a speaking to God with our hearts, the Spirit works within us to enlighten us to understand the Word of God and the will of God.

The Holy Spirit moves believers to pray. This work of the Spirit gives believers confidence in praying to God. If the Spirit knows the will of God and if the Spirit moves believers to pray according to God's will, then believers can

22. Lang, "Martin Bucer," 161.

pray with all confidence and assurance that God will hear and answer prayers. In this way, Christians grow in their lives of faith.

Christians live their whole lives in dependence on God. They seek to discern God's will with the help of God's Spirit. Believers bring before God those requests they believe to be in accord with God's will. Beyond what they ask is their constant prayer that all their requests will be an expression of God's will and will bring God glory. Bucer urged Christians always to pray, as did Jesus: "nevertheless, Father, not my will, but thine be done" (Luke 22:42).

Bucer's summary for Christians who pray consisted of four points: 1) Pray by the Spirit. 2) Through the Spirit, be certain that what one prays for is to the glory of God. 3) Be persuaded, through the Holy Spirit, that God will answer your prayers. 4) Pray with humility trusting God will gladly answer your prayers and believing God is pleased to do so. These four prescriptions continue to be important ways for Christians to grow in faith as they daily commune with God in prayer. The essence of prayer for Bucer is always to pray in the Spirit and pray for the Spirit. For our lives as Christians are possible only in the Spirit of God.

QUESTIONS FOR DISCUSSION

1. Why is it important to recognize the important work of the Holy Spirit in salvation?

2. What are ways the Holy Spirit helps us interpret the Bible?

3. In what ways does the Holy Spirit guide the church? Your Christian life?

4. What is the role of the Holy Spirit in Christian prayer?

6

SIN AND SALVATION

Central to the biblical story are the themes of sin and salvation. We are introduced to the concept of sin in Genesis 3 when Adam and Eve disobeyed God. We hear of salvation in the Bible's most famous verse, John 3:16.

In between these verses—and beyond—sin and salvation represent the two dimensions of life for humans: we are people of sin; or we are people of salvation.

SIN

Martin Bucer, in line with the historic Christian theological tradition, stressed the sinfulness of all human beings (Rom 3:23). Sin takes many forms and expressions. Bucer spoke of sin as being that which is contrary to God's law; "evil counsels and designs of the mind"; failure to worship and love "God the creator with the total devotion that is his right"; "evil desire" and, in essence, alienation from God. This is the basic condition of sin, which affects all people.

In his commentary on Romans (on 5:18–21), Bucer went on to describe ways the apostle Paul describes the sin from which Christ has cleansed us and for which Christ imparts God's righteousness to sinners. Sin and salvation.

Original Sin

Bucer writes that, from the story in Genesis, there is sin that "Adam transmitted to his posterity. We call it original sin, because it issues from our first origin, having been dispersed from our first parent among all his progeny."[1] Sin emerges in the origins of the human race. It is now of the nature of all who are born. It is a reality as much as are our physical characteristics.

Sin defines the "human condition." This sin, said Bucer, is "neither deed nor word nor thought, but the corruption of judgment and desire whence proceed all evil thoughts and words and deeds." Sin corrupts the human being in relation to God. All human judgments and desires express themselves in the evil thoughts and words and deeds that express the corrupted nature of the human person. This emerges from "one man" and brought death which "spread to all" (Rom 5:12ff.). Even before the law of God was given (The Ten Commandments—Exod 20)—which is the standard by which sin is measured when commandments are broken—prior to the law, sin is present and exercised power over all persons. The law of God brings a clear recognition of what sinful nature of humans lead to in terms of actions and behavior.

From various Scripture passages (e.g., Rom 7; 1 Cor 2; Eph 2), the grim—and deadly—picture of sin emerges. From "our first beginnings," said Bucer, "we have been tainted and sold under sin and consequently are held subject to

1. Bucer, *Common Places*, 121.

the kingdom of Satan and the wrath of God."[2] In relation to a holy God who created humans in the divine image (Gen 1:26–27), sin deserves God's judgment. Sinners do not seek to obey God or God's will for their lives. Bucer wrote:

> It is quite obvious to all who seek straightforwardly to believe the word of God, that original sin is the infection and corruption of the whole man which prevents him recognising and aspiring after God and his will as the truest good; instead his judgment on anything is warped, he regards and desires nothing in its proper place and rank, but abuses and perverts all things.[3]

The pervasiveness of sin means the totality of a human's existence is affected. In relation to God, humans are "dead through trespasses and sins" (Eph 2:1; Col 2:13). The corruption of human nature infects all and prevents all persons from seeking God. Sin prevents us from doing God's will as the way to live according to the divine image in which we are created. Original sin affects our whole human existence making our judgment on anything "warped," causing us to seek our own ways and wills instead of God's way and will for our lives. In relation to God, we are alienated and sinful in God's sight.

The universality of sin as alienation from God which radically affects all humans is consistent with the teachings of Augustine (354–430). Followers of Pelagius (354–418) taught that sin did not corrupt human nature but rather that humans were autonomous and could freely choose whether to sin or not to sin. As Bucer summarized Pelagian views: "The Pelagians' denial of original sin is beyond dispute; hence they understand the apostle's statement on the

2. Bucer, *Common Places*, 122.

3. Bucer, *Common Places*, 122.

subject in this chapter [Rom. 5]—that by one man sin came into the world, and transmitted death to all men—to mean only the fact that Adam bequeathed the example of sinning to his descendants."[4]

Bucer maintained, as did other sixteenth-century Protestant reformers, that humanity's ruin and condemnation before God is the human condition and that all persons are sinners by nature. We are "utterly undone through ignorance of God and a frantic covetousness for the things that this life provides."[5] God, said Bucer, "justly condemns those who are evil by nature."[6] Sin is *serious*.

Free Will

The radical effects of sin found in all humans, being sinners by nature, raises questions about what humans can do—or cannot do—in relation to any change in our sinful condition. In what ways can human sin be forgiven? How can humans be reconciled with God? How can human beings be "justified" in the sight of God—how can humans be saved and receive the salvation of which the Scriptures speak?

The term "free will" becomes part of this discussion. When we hear this term, we realize it can be understood in different senses.

"Free will" can refer to how humans may act in their everyday life. Humans make decisions. They act in accord with their choices. They can choose, for example, either to pick up a pen or not pick up a pen.

We can say God is at work as the "first cause" of all actions, as Bucer notes. But

4. Bucer, *Common Places*, 124.

5. Bucer, *Common Places*, 125.

6. Bucer, *Common Places*, 126.

a first cause does not preclude the functioning of second causes. God does indeed act in us in everything, and acts upon us too according to his good pleasure, but he does so in such a way that he causes us to act, so that by his action we come to understand an issue, exercise choice, accept or reject, and set our physical powers in motion.[7]

On the "human level," humans can freely decide one way or another on their actions. They do so freely and in that sense, we have "free will." As Bucer put it: "By "free will," then, we mean simply the faculty or choosing or rejecting the things that come our way, in accordance with our decided judgment. This faculty is called 'free will' according to its natural meaning."[8]

But when we contemplate "the range of this faculty, how far our free will extends," as Bucer said, "we must in the end confess that of itself our free will is of no avail for the appropriation of the things that belong to true godliness, but only for their refusal and rejection."[9] When it comes to theological things, the "things of God" or obeying God, then we find that—because of sin: "without the Spirit of Christ to renew and energise the whole man, it is completely powerless in relation to what is truly profitable, that is, what renders us acceptable to God and constitutes the life of righteousness."[10]

Bucer continued to say that "the free will that has not been born again is of no avail at all in regard to what commends us in the sight of God." For "the free will that is left to itself always rejects and never desires the things of God and

7. Bucer, *Common Places*, 146.

8. Bucer, *Common Places*, 147.

9. Bucer, *Common Places*, 148.

10. Bucer, *Common Places*, 149.

of true godliness, for godliness conflicts with what it desires. From infancy the human heart is corrupt and intent on perverse ways." For the human will cannot "appropriate true godliness" unless it is "sustained and moved by the Spirit of Christ. For as long as the Spirit is lacking the man is dead in his sins, bereft of every awareness of true life, and is moreover moved by an evil spirit, the instigator of all offences, who 'is at work in the children of disobedience' [Eph. 2:2]."[11]

True freedom of the will can come only by the work of the Spirit of God. Like Augustine, Bucer acknowledged that "unless God turns and draws us to himself, unless he lives his life in us and perfects it for us, we can neither turn and come to him, nor live his life, let alone carry it to perfection."[12] In short, said Bucer, "we ascribe everything to God and acknowledge and confess in accordance with his word that whatever we do aright, such as it is, is his gift and work in us."

SALVATION

Humans are sinners by nature, cut off from God. We are under God's judgment and unable to establish a loving, trusting relationship with God, our creator. Bucer's emphasis on original sin and our lack of true freedom to choose to love and serve God leaves humans in the position of being unable to save themselves. We cannot "lift ourselves up by our own bootstraps" and present ourselves with any merit or goodness to God. If there is to be any "salvation" or new relationship with God—it must be *God* who provides it for sinful persons!

11. Bucer, *Common Places*, 150.

12. Bucer, *Common Places*, 152.

Election and Predestination

Central to Bucer's theology were the doctrines of election and predestination. These doctrines provided Bucer's understandings of the way humans can be saved, through the gift of salvation given by God in choosing to save us in Jesus Christ.

Bucer indicated that "predestination" comes from the Greek word *proorismos* which literally means "predetermination." He wrote that

> "Predestination" is that act of designation on the part of God whereby in his secret counsel he designates and actually selects and separates from the rest of mankind those whom he will draw to his Son, Jesus our Lord, and ingraft them into him (having brought them into this life at his own good time), and whom, when thus drawn and ingrafted, he will regenerate through Christ and will sanctify to fulfil his purposes. This, then, as I have said, is the predestination of the saints.[13]

This action of predestination rests completely on God's free decision. Through the death of Christ, the "elect" are saved, regenerated, and given the gift of salvation in Christ.

This election or choosing by God, said Bucer, indicates "the certainty of God's goodwill towards his saints, and hence the divine predestination of which he is speaking here [Ephesians 1] is the marking out of the saints for participation in salvation."[14] Predestination is "the election and destining of the saints for eternal salvation."[15]

---

13. Bucer, *Common Places*, 96. The two groups in predestination are the "elect" and the "reprobate."

14. Bucer, *Common Places*, 97.

15. Bucer, *Common Places*, 99.

In Bucer's theology, election and predestination point to two realities. One is, negatively, to say that no human works contribute to human salvation. The positive dimension is that salvation depends totally on God's gracious, free election.

Due to human sin, humans have no ability to do good or choose anything other than sinful actions in relation to God. Predestination indicates that for salvation, all is to be ascribed to God's goodness and nothing to ourselves, or any "merit" we think we may achieve. Humans are "dead through trespasses and sins" (Eph 2:1; Col 2:13). They can contribute nothing to their salvation. Only God's Holy Spirit can bring the gift of faith and new life in Jesus Christ (see chapter 5 above). Salvation is accomplished by God through the death of God's Son (Rom 5:8). Humans are unable to earn their salvation and can receive the new life of faith only by God's gracious choosing (predestination). Bucer quoted Philip Melanchthon to indicate we should consider predestination "solely in order that you may be more certain of your salvation and may cleave more firmly to the promises of God."[16]

Importantly, Bucer stressed that God's election is carried out "through Jesus Christ." God "elected and predestined us in and through Christ before the foundation of the world" (Eph 1:4; cf. John 17:24; 1 Pet 1:20). This election is not by human merit, only by the merit of Christ's blood (Eph 1:7; 2:13). The centrality of Christ and Christ's death as the means by which one's election is carried out focuses election for persons in a very personal way. We are not to lie awake at night worrying about whether we are "elect." Instead, one must only ask: Do I believe in Jesus Christ and that by his death on the cross, I can be saved? Election is

16. Bucer was citing Melanchthon's, *Loci Communes* (1535), in the section "On Predestination." *Common Places*, 99.

focused in the work of Christ. For persons concerned with salvation, the question is: "Do I believe in Christ?" If the answer is "yes," it can indicate they have received the gift of faith by the Holy Spirit and will be of the elect of God. Bucer spoke directly about this when he wrote:

> The first demand God makes of us is to believe that he is God, that is, the Saviour, so that when we hear him summoning to himself all who are afflicted and distressed [Matt. 11:28] we hasten eagerly to him. Now if those whom God calls heed his call, he has assuredly predestined and foreknown them, and will also justify and glorify them. Therefore, the first duty you owe to God is to believe that you have been predestined by him, because unless you believe that, you represent him as making sport of you when he calls you to salvation through the gospel. For by the gospel he summons you to justification and to share his glory, but these can be experienced only by those who have been predestined, foreknown and elected to do so.[17]

God's predestination grounds salvation not in human efforts but in the election and call of God to believe in Jesus Christ. Response to the gospel message of salvation in Christ enables one to believe one is predestined and receives salvation (by the work of the Holy Spirit). "For it is true believers who have eternal life," said Bucer, and "they can no more doubt that they have it than doubt the Lord's promise that He who believes in me has eternal life" (John 3:15).[18]

This promise is important since it is a ground of assurance. We can believe the true promise of eternal life as

17. Bucer, *Common Places*, 99.

18. Bucer, *Common Places*, 100.

coming by faith in Jesus Christ—the gift given us by the Holy Spirit. Assurance of salvation is from God's promise in Christ. Said Bucer:

> Because all our righteousness is so maimed and mutilated that by its merit alone we could never be assured of our salvation (for it fails to satisfy the law of God), assurance of our predestination and election is to be sought only from the promise and calling of God, and our attention must always be directed away from our own righteousness, which of itself is permanently an abomination in the sight of God, towards the divine promise.[19]

Predestination or election is saying that salvation in Jesus Christ is by God's grace alone. For "election is the pure gift of God; therefore it is grace, not reward."[20]

Bucer said, "Election is the designation by the pure grace of God, of some out of the general mass of lost mankind, to attain to the knowledge of the will of God and finally to eternal life."[21] Since we are saved through Jesus Christ, "our mediator is eternal, and we are eternally united with Him; our union with Christ is unbreakable and cannot be other than everlasting."[22] "On account of the merit of Christ we are considered blameless, and our imperfection is forgiven—rather it is even made perfect. Our purity stands in this, that God has absolved us through Christ; therefore none of the elect can be condemned. Where there is remission of sins, there is faith, adoption, salvation, and perfect purity, imparted by God and received by us through

---

19. Bucer, *Common Places*, 101.

20. Bucer, *Common Places*, 114.

21. Bucer, *Common Places*, 111.

22. Bucer, *Common Places*, 112.

Christ."[23] "The goal of election," said Bucer, "is that we should know God, love and worship him, and live according to his will."[24]

Justification by Faith

The goal of election in God's granting salvation by grace is realized theologically through justification by faith. This is a biblical image of salvation and one to which Bucer devoted much attention.

Built on biblical terms and usage, Bucer defined justification as meaning "God's acquitting us and deciding our case in our favour when our own thoughts and Satan accuse us."[25] Justification grants the "certainty that God is gracious towards us, forgives the sins which never fail to oppress us, and counts us among his own people." In short, justification assures us in "our knowing first of all that we have a God peacefully disposed towards us."

Justification relates to righteousness. As sinners, no one is righteous before God who is righteousness itself. "There is no one who does good, no, not one" (Ps 14:3; cf. 53:3) sums up the biblical view. As Bucer put it, "Our natural constitution is such that we are powerless to serve others and manifest God's likeness."[26] Bucer speaks of justification as *both* the "imputing" of righteousness *and* the "impartation" righteousness. In justification, the righteousness of Jesus Christ—who is fully and ever without sin is imputed to the sinner. Before God, the sinner stands—not as a sinner—but clothed in the righteousness of Christ. The righteousness of Christ is "imputed" or given to the

23. Bucer, *Common Places*, 113.

24. Bucer, *Common Places*, 111.

25. Bucer, *Common Places*, 161.

26. Bucer, *Common Places*, 161.

"account" of the sinner. When God imputes righteousness this way, God also "imparts" righteousness to the sinner by the power of the Holy Spirit, which now is given to the justified sinner. Bucer wrote: the word "justify" means

> that righteousness which God produces by his Spirit in those who believe in Christ, and which he intends to be his attestation to the effect that he has now forgiven their sins and counts them among those he resolved to justify, that is, to count among the righteous not only by pardoning their sin but also by conforming them to the image of his Son.[27]

God "justifies the ungodly" (Rom 4:5). God both forgives and renews!

We are justified by faith (Rom 3:28; 5:1). Bucer defined faith as "the sure persuasion through the Holy Spirit of God's love and fatherly kindness towards us, in reliance upon our Lord Jesus Christ, who by his death has expiated our sins, and by his life through which he now reigns, makes us partakers of his righteousness."[28] Likewise, Bucer said faith was "an unwavering persuasion of God's mercy and fatherly kindness towards us, created through the Holy Spirit and resting on the accepted sacrifice of Christ."[29]

Faith given by the Holy Spirit is focused on Jesus Christ and his death. Through Christ crucified, our sin is atoned for and forgiven ("expiated"). Christ's death is called a "sacrifice." Bucer did not seek to explain *how* the death of Christ brings forgiveness of sin and atonement—the

27. Bucer, *Common Places*, 163. Justification occurs at the beginning of our salvation. It consists of God forgiving our sin by grace and granting to us the righteousness of Jesus Christ to be our own. We receive Christ's righteousness when we believe in him.

28. Bucer, *Common Places*, 196.

29. Bucer, *Common Places*, 172.

coming together of God and humanity in reconciliation. Other theologians have developed "theories of the atonement" to provide potential explanations of how Christ's death brings atonement and salvation.[30] But for Bucer, it was enough just to indicate that Christ's death brings forgiveness, reconciliation, and salvation. Bucer wrote that the terms "faith" and "believe"—when we speak of our being "justified by faith" and that "salvation is granted to believers"—mean "a sure assent to the promises in which God pledges us, on account of his Son's death, the pardon of our sins, the Spirit of righteousness, and eternal life."[31]

Justification brings us the experience of God's merciful favor. For Bucer, "surely no godly soul can doubt for a moment that it is through God's mercy alone and for the sake of Christ's merit alone that we are justified, pronounced righteous before God, and not because of anything in us at all, however many works of holiness, however genuine our fruits of the Spirit."[32]

Justification by faith does bring effects. Bucer saw these as that of

> begetting virtues and good works, an effect which is at the same time assured, and of even greater power, and in this manner we reject the unjust allegation that we are undermining good works. . . . So far from denying thereby that the sum and substance of justification is the free remission of our sins and our acceptance before God for the sake of our Lord Jesus Christ, on

30. One study of theological views is McDonald, *The Atonement*.

31. Bucer, *Common Places*, 173. Bucer said that our "assent" to God's promises in faith is "not merely an act of the understanding but also of the will."

32. Bucer, *Common Places*, 164.

which faith exclusively relies, we even establish
the point more strongly than ever.[33]

Good works follow justification and depend on justification. They are the gifts of God and the fruits of the Holy Spirit in those who are justified by divine grace. They are done for the sake of Jesus Christ as expressions of love and commitment to him.

Justification is by faith, not works (Gal 2:16; 3:11). But justification leads the justified to do good works. The Holy Spirit given to those justified (the elect) leads believers into new life, lived in conformity with the image of Christ. This is God's purpose in election; and for this purpose God gives the Holy Spirit to those who have received faith by the Spirit. Good works do not *cause* justification by faith. Good works *testify to* justification by faith.

In summary: justification is "the heart of our salvation" which Bucer fully defines as "our free acceptance before God, whereby he pardons our sins, imputes righteousness to us, and bestows on us eternal life; this life is begun here and now and daily increased in us by the Spirit, who is the implanter and cultivator of righteousness and good works."[34] Faith is not our human work. For no one can believe in Christ and Christ's death without illumination by the Holy Spirit. The Spirit is given to the elect of God, those chosen "before the foundation of the world" (Eph 1:4). Faith is the work of God in us—the God who is gracious to us on account of Christ's merit in his sacrificial death on the cross. For Bucer, all things that pertain to our salvation is God's gift, the free work of God's spontaneous goodness to us.[35] To God be the glory!

33. Bucer, *Common Places*, 166.

34. Bucer, *Common Places*, 167.

35. In his lectures on Ephesians, Bucer wrote that being justified by faith is about receiving, not giving, not doing. It is about

QUESTIONS FOR DISCUSSION

1. What evidence is there that humans are sinful?

2. Why was important for Bucer to recognize that humans cannot by their own "free will" respond positively to gospel of Jesus Christ?

3. What is the role of election and predestination in salvation?

4. What is the role of Jesus Christ in justification by faith?

---

accepting—not trying to gain God's good will toward us—but receiving God's gift in Jesus Christ which is already prepared for us.

7

CHURCH AND MINISTRY

CHURCH

Martin Bucer defined the church very simply as "the body of Christ" (1 Cor 12:27). This means, wrote Bucer, that the church is a "company" of people "governed by the Spirit and word of Christ, just as our whole body is governed by the head. For this reason it consists only of the elect and regenerate, and rightly comprises all who are united together in Christ, whether in heaven or on earth (so in Hebrews 12 it is called "the heavenly Jerusalem," etc. [12:22f.]), and is known to God alone."[1] God's purpose in election is to impart the Holy Spirit to the elect and give them new life through faith.

Bucer emphasized "there is no Church without faith, and no faith apart from the word. All the saints of every age have been born again by the word."[2] The church is born

---

1. Bucer, *Common Places*, 202. One scholar wrote that "Bucer's theology was a theology of the Church." See Stupperich, "Martin Bucer als Theologe und Kirchenmann," 254. Cited in Lugioyo, *Martin Bucer's Doctrine of Justification*, 5.

2. Bucer, *Common Places*, 215.

through the living Word God speaks to the human heart. Put personally, for Bucer, Christ receives poor sinners and joins them into a beloved community for whom Christ intercedes (Rom 8:26). The Holy Spirit unites those who believe in Christ and holds them together in one body (1 Cor 12:13; Eph 4:4). By Word, Sacrament, and church discipline the Spirit builds up the church and builds up Christians in faith. The Spirit binds the church together.

The church is universal. It is "the Church of all who have been born again by true faith and are here on earth absent from the Lord."[3] The church extends throughout the world since the church is also "local." It is "assemblies of people in particular regions, cities, parishes, families, and houses, who by the same faith call upon and worship the same God."[4] These gatherings constitute the universal church, expressed in numerous places. In all expressions, the church recognizes "none of the earthly members of the Church becomes its head; it has its head in Christ in heaven. . . . Christ himself is alone its ruler and governor."[5] Christ uses humans to carry out the church's ministries while always knowing the church is "never bereft of the presence of Christ himself with his own." Bucer went on to say that Christ "cleanses the Church with his own blood, quickens it by his own Spirit, and although he makes use of various ministries in it, yet he is himself its first and foremost and most powerful minister."[6]

Bucer was a realist about the church on earth, recognizing—as had Augustine—that the church here "is always mixed, containing sheep, that is, saints, and goats,

---

3. Bucer, *Common Places*, 202.

4. Bucer, *Common Places*, 203.

5. Bucer, *Common Places*, 203.

6. Bucer, *Common Places*, 204.

hypocrites."[7] When the goats and hypocrites "betray their ungodliness, they must be disciplined" by the church, a function which it is necessary for the church to carry out.[8] This led Bucer to list five "marks" without which, he said, there cannot be a Church."[9] These are:

1. Heed is paid to the voice of its Shepherd

2. The ministry of teaching

3. The possession of suitable minister and teachers of the Word, faithful stewards of the mysteries of God.

4. The lawful dispensation of the Sacraments.

5. Righteousness and holiness of life.

"The Church which lacks these aforesaid marks," said Bucer, "is not to be called the body of Christ. Although it may contain many members of Christ, it is not a fellowship gathered by the Spirit of Christ, comprising [clergy], ministers and people."[10]

These marks of the church, found in individual congregations, point to the church's overall unity. The unity of the church consists, Bucer maintains, in "the unity of the Spirit, of love, the word of God, Christ, the sacraments, and the sharing of gifts, that we may aspire together to the same goal, and hold and express the same beliefs."[11] The Spirit binds the church together in Jesus Christ, as Ephesians 4:1–6 makes clear. Bucer wrote: "One word, one Scripture, one baptism, one death of Christ, one Father, one worship, one love, the same sacrament of the eucharist, the same

7. Bucer, *Common Places*, 204.

8. Bucer, *Common Places*, 205.

9. Bucer, *Common Places*, 205. Or, "the church cannot exist." These marks are listed and discussed on pages 205–6.

10. Bucer, *Common Places*, 206.

11. Bucer, *Common Places*, 208.

laying-on of hands, the same discipline, and the agreement of ministers, and of those to whom these things are ministered—in short, it is essential that we hold completely in common everything instituted for the building up of the Church."[12] The church's unity is theological. Essential beliefs and practices are joined as expressions of the unity God has established in the church, in Jesus Christ, by the power of the Holy Spirit. These theological convictions led Bucer throughout his life as a reformer to be "A Champion of Protestant Unity."[13]

While theological unity is essential, Bucer also maintained that unity is not necessary in anything not set forth in the Word; here a degree of liberty obtains. So in the matter of man-made rites, different arrangements can be made in different quarters the better suited to edification. To meet the different needs of the time, we introduce non-essential practices to fulfil essential requirements. So different churches have instituted practices varying in respect of place, occasion, method, and form of words.[14]

Local needs can be met in "non-essential" practices. A certain "contextualization" is necessary to be responsive to particular situations in churches.

Bucer outlines church "observances" in three "classes."

1. Those observances for which "Scripture contains explicit instructions."

2. Those which are "not explicitly prescribed by Scripture" but which can be shown to be "in accordance with Scripture." Examples are the baptism of infants, the

---

12. Bucer, *Common Places*, 208.

13. This is Greschat's title for chapter 5 in his *Martin Bucer*. Along similar lines, David Wright introduces Bucer's *Common Places* with an essay: "Martin Bucer: Ecumenical Theologian."

14. Bucer, *Common Places*, 208.

hallowing of the Lord's Day, admission of women to the Lord's Supper, etc.

3. Practices instituted by church leaders. Examples are "forms of prayer, the times of fasting, lectionary arrangements," etc. As long as these "do not militate against the divine will but rather have its promotion as their object and also have regard to complete doctrinal purity, observances in this class may be free from restrictions, saving of course the maintenance of peace and love."[15]

These delineations of the different classes of observances or church practices show Bucer's concern to honor the place of the church in God's work and as the means by which God's will and work is carried out. The church is the instrument of God in the proclamation of the gospel. The goal of seeking others as "lost sheep" is to bring them into Christ's "fold." These are those who commit themselves fully to Christ, they hear his voice and use what God has given to bring others to Christ. It is only in this community of Christ that salvation is received and lived out (John 10:7–18).

The church has an essential role in God's work and in making God's work known to the world. The church is the context in which the Holy Spirit works to enable believers in the church to serve God and serve others. Bucer put this recognition in personal terms in his *Catechism* when he said Christians should:

> Confess that I am one who gathers for Christ's word and sacrament; that I receive the forgiveness of sins and all good. I give myself wholly to such a congregation and will attend to hearing the Gospel preached in sermons with complete reverence and obedience as well as receiving the holy sacraments (at the appointed time). I will be a faithful and obedient member with all who

15. Bucer, *Common Places*, 210.

call on the name of our Lord Jesus. I will allow myself to be taught, urged, and disciplined and will show that to all others in love and humility.[16]

MINISTRY

Ministry of Love

Bucer held fast to the theological unity of the church under its head, Jesus Christ. But he acknowledged the flexibility the church must have to carry out its work in ways that can enhance its ministries by practices and observances that, growing out of Scripture, can keep the church's theology pure. Importantly, he urged in all such practices there must be a continuing "maintenance of peace and love."

The church is the fellowship (Greek: *koinonia*) of saints when, as Bucer writes: "all are devoted to God and their neighbour, and committed with total dedication to the holy ordinances of the Church."[17] Fellowship was "a conspicuous feature of the primitive Church," said Bucer, "and is so still wherever such love abounds that those who have the same God and Christ also share with each other whatever spiritual or temporal goods they have received from God."[18] In this, "the whole Church is thereby bound together by the firmest and finest of bonds, and the distinctiveness and differences of ministries and ministers are preserved." Fellowship in the Spirit is "an active kindness whereby according to our ability we contribute from the whole of our material possessions to all, even the absent, according to their needs. The level of need is the measure of

16. Bucer, cited in Stephens, *The Holy Spirit in the Theology of Martin Bucer*, 161.

17. Bucer, *Common Places*, 210.

18. Bucer, *Common Places*, 210.

such sharing."[19] The church shows the marks of the Spirit's work among the elect as the body of Christ. It is not "church membership" or baptism that constitutes the church's life. Rather, the true church is the elect who are living in the Spirit's presence by faith as marked by the Word and Sacraments and righteousness of life.

Bucer emphasized that in the church, ministry takes place as the children of God recognize others as their brothers and sisters and serve them in love. Theologically, "the relationship of the church to Christ and the Spirit, and the interrelation of election, faith, and holiness, mean that the church as the elect is marked positively by the presence of the Spirit and the love of one's neighbour, and negatively by their absence or, indeed, by the sin against the Holy Spirit."[20] This expresses Bucer's emphases that faith is always active in love (Gal 5:6) and that a failure of love is the result of a lack of faith.[21] Love is always the companion of true faith, a fruit of the Spirit, and love will be expressed to others by those in the church.

Shortly after Bucer arrived in Strasbourg, he wrote *That No One Should Live for Himself but for Others, and How to Attain to This Ideal* (1523).[22] Here Bucer said that

> No one should live for himself, because God has created all things so that they might contribute not to their own good but to that of others, and be instruments and evidences of the divine goodness which all things should express and

19. Bucer, *Common Places*, 211.

20. Stephens, "The Church in Bucer's Commentaries on the Epistle to the Ephesians," 49.

21. Cf. Stephens, "The Church in Bucer's Commentaries on the Epistle to the Ephesians," 58.

22. This work was translated as *Instruction in Love, by Martin Bucer, the Reformer*, trans. Fuhrmann.

spread abroad. The Lord God first established this order of things at the time of creation, and will bring it about again at the time of the renovation of the world when he will again bring in his kingdom.[23]

Bucer continued to say that "the best, the most perfect and blessed condition on earth is that in which a man can usefully and profitably serve his neighbor."[24] "Living not for our own benefit but for that of others, and for the glory of God," said Bucer, is not possible by human efforts. "To put it briefly, only Faith can bring and impart such a life to us."[25] For "faith not only brings into us a complete trust in Christ, but it also restores us to that right and divine order in which we were created. Moreover, through faith we are offered and accept his Spirit which makes us certain that we are the children of God. As a result we gladly do all kinds of deeds of love for our neighbor."[26] "True faith," said Bucer, "surely brings true love which makes us overflow with good works toward our neighbor, and live not for ourselves but for the eternal glory of God."[27]

The ministry of love is carried out by all Christians in the believing community. The Spirit works in each believer in the fellowship of the church. As Lang put it: "Christ works in each elect individual, and each individual, with

23. Bucer, *Instruction in Love*, 28.

24. Bucer, *Instruction in Love*, 30.

25. Bucer, *Instruction in Love*, 42.

26. Bucer, *Instruction in Love*, 46.

27. Bucer, *Instruction in Love*, 51. In summary: "True faith is that through which we come to live not for ourselves but for others to the glory of God, and to be assiduous in truly good works" (50–51). Bucer concluded his work by saying: "The divine Word brings faith; faith brings love; love brings good deeds as its fruit—after which God gives us the eternal inheritance, a wholly divine and blessed life. Amen" (52).

his special gift, is an instrument of the Holy Spirit. Thus, through Christ's Word and Spirit, there arises the care of souls and the disciplined fellowship in which each member recognizes it as his special task not only to see to his own growth in grace, but also to the salvation and edification of his neighbor's soul."[28] The ministry of love includes "the care of souls." Bucer was already to remind believers to pray for their neighbors.[29] Believers will be open and sensitive to the promptings and moving of the Spirit as they carry out their ministries in serving others in love. For Bucer, "Those who hear Christ and the Holy Spirit are eager to undertake and perform all good deeds in that order and manner which they acknowledge to have been determined for them by the Lord and the Holy Spirit."[30] Bucer made this comment in the midst of his discussion of a "proper observance" of "all the churches" and "the Kingdom of Christ is the care for the poor and needy. For the Lord expressly forbids his people to allow anyone among them to be in need (Deut. 15:4)."[31] The ministries of love express care for the spiritual lives of others as well as for their physical needs—the strong admonition being given to care for the poor and needy.

Ministry of the Word

The ministry of the church in its varied forms is guided by the Holy Spirit. The Spirit calls, equips, guides, and uses ministers of the Word (and Sacrament) to proclaim the Word of God, which is the means by which salvation is

28. Lang, "Martin Bucer," 161.

29. Bucer taught the four parts of prayer to be adoration, confession, thanksgiving, and supplication for neighbors. See Amos, *Bucer, Ephesians and Biblical Humanism,* 198.

30. Bucer, *De Regno Christi,* 267.

31. Bucer, *De Regno Christi,* 256.

made known to the world. Since "faith comes from what is heard, and what is heard comes through the word of Christ" (Rom 10:17), the ministry of the Word is necessary—and crucial—to the life of the church. Preaching is important. The Spirit speaks through ministers of the Word in preaching and brings efficacy to the preached Word, making preaching effective in making known Jesus Christ as Lord and Savior. Bucer believe that when those who are Christ's speak, it is not they who speak, but the Spirit of God who speaks in them.

The work of preaching is used by God, through the Holy Spirit, to convey God's message. God chooses those who will minister in this way. They use their gifts and talents for the preaching task. But beyond the preacher is the divine activity of God the Holy Spirit who "opens the ears" of those who hear Christian proclamation to come to faith by illuminating their hearts and minds to receive the gospel of Christ by faith. God uses human messengers to convey the divine message.

Over-against Anabaptist views that God did not need an established, "ordained" ministry; and Roman Catholic views that the church's sacraments are inherently effective for those who receive them in good standing in the church, Bucer's emphasis on the Spirit's work in using the human labors of preachers whose preaching becomes a "means of grace" to those who hear—and respond, by the Spirit—was important.[32] God uses human preachers as interpreters of the Word of God. The preacher's words are energized and made effectual and effective in the lives of their hearers by

---

32. More generally, Ian Hazlett points out that "Bucer increasingly thought more positively about ministry, external Word, and sacrament in the visible church, as 'means of grace' for true believers—if fanned by the Spirit." See Hazlett, "Bucer" in *The Cambridge Companion*, 110.

the work of the Holy Spirit. Preaching is not "automatic" and is entirely "necessary."

Bucer maintained the freedom of God in preaching. God and God's work is not limited to the work of the preacher. God's Spirit is free to work when and how and where God wills. Yet "God decided, through the foolishness of our proclamation, to save those who believe" (1 Cor 1:21). Preachers can preach, but it is *God*, through the Spirit, who brings the increase and establishes faith. Preaching is not in vain for it is the divinely sanctioned way of spreading the Word of God. Bucer said that God sees to it that those sent by God are heard and received. Most broadly, ministry is effective when and how God wills.

Bucer's emphases on these issues recognizes that the minister possesses no inherent power within their person. It is *Christ* who breathes the Holy Spirit to those who proclaim salvation to the word. This proclamation takes place not by the minister's own powers but by the power of the Spirit of whom "breath" is a symbol of the divine presence. The ministry is a work of the whole Trinity. At different times, salvation is expressed as the work of the Father, the Son, and the Holy Spirit. But the ministry of salvation is always God's work, not a human work—however much God uses persons as divine representatives. God is not bound to human means to save the elect, to any human works, or to any words or actions (signs) administered by human ministers.

Ministry of Order and Discipline

The church's ministry includes the ministries of the preachers and teachers of the Word and the people of God who live out their faith through good works, particularly works of love.

Within the church itself, Bucer recognized church order as being constituted by four offices: pastors, teachers, elders, and deacons.[33] Each had functions so the church's ministries could be carried out in an orderly manner.[34] Those who exercise these ministries do so for the common good and for the church's unity and for the spreading of love.

Pastors preach the Word of God and offer pastoral care. In 1538, Bucer wrote *Von der waren Seelsorge—On the True Pastoral Care*—which has been called his "masterwork of pastoral theology."[35] This book was an extended commentary on scriptural passages. Pastoral care is the application of Scripture to life. Bucer's key text was Ezekiel 34:16: "I will seek the lost, and I will bring back the strayed, and I will bind up the injured, and I will strengthen the weak." He took his paradigm from this sheepfold metaphor and identified five tasks of the pastor in the care of souls: to search for the lost; bring back strays; bind up wounded sheep (those who have strayed into sin); strengthen the weak; and to guard and feed the healthy sheep. Bucer commented

33. In this, Bucer had an influence on John Calvin, who spent time as a minister in Strasbourg. See de Kroon and van't Spijker, *Martin Bucer,* 155–68. Cf. Marijn de Kroon, *Martin Bucer und Johannes Calvin.*

34. Elsie Anne McKee has written: "A four-fold ministry has come to be considered characteristic of the Reformed Church, and modern scholarship has traced this paradigm to Martin Bucer, from whom Calvin adopted it. In this case, the pastoral order is seen as including doctors or teachers. In fact, however, although the educational interest was vital and never lost, doctors were a distinct office only in Geneva. There is some debate as to whether the four-fold office was ever really effected. Certainly in Bucer's Strasbourg it was more theory than practice, though it is commonly conceded that Calvin approximated the ideal more closely in his later years in Geneva." McKee, *John Calvin on the Diaconate,* 135.

35. See Burnett, *The Yoke of Christ,* 87.

on Scripture passages and reflected on them, pastorally. He sought to deal not only with the letter of Scripture but also with Scripture's "true spirit and the power of the Lord." Bucer moved to Christ's lordship over the church through its various ministries. The Christian life is lived "in Christ" and all things are to be subordinated to Christ.[36]

Elders (presbyters), wrote Bucer are those "specially endowed with a spirit of discernment and religious zeal, who supervise Church discipline along with the minsters of the word and sacraments."[37] Bucer wrote further in his *De Regno Christi* that the duties of elders were

> to exercise discipline, to admonish brethren of their duty both privately and in their own homes, and when anyone has to be admonished in the name of the Church or corrected or bound over to penance or excommunicated, to be present, and to pronounce sentence wholesomely, and truly to manifest themselves to these as apt teachers (I Tim. 3:2), i.e., fit and eager to teach and tenacious and faithful of expression in teaching, and strong in exhorting through sound doctrine, and also in reclaiming those who deny the truth (Titus 1:9).[38]

36. On these points see Purves, *Pastoral Theology*, 84–85.

37. Bucer, *Common Places*, 259. A fuller picture of church discipline is found in Burnett, "Church Discipline and Moral Reformation in the Thought of Martin Bucer."

38. Bucer, *De Regno Christi*, 231. Wilhelm Pauck noted that for Bucer: "The ministry of the Church as he conceived it and as he hoped to establish it in Strassburg (and, according to his recommendations in this work, also in England) was to consist of the offices of preaching and teaching elders, trained for their tasks; untrained lay elders who, together with the older ministers, would be responsible for the administration of discipline; and deacons who would be in charge of poor relief and the administration of benevolences. Calvin's conception of the ministry was similar (cf. Calvin, *Institutes* IV. xi. 1 and 6; and IV. iv. 2)." Bucer, *De Regno Christi*, 231 n. 35.

Deacons, said Bucer, while they may assist the elders in helping with "the discipline of Christ and the administration of the sacraments, it was their principal duty to keep a list of all of Christ's needy in the churches, to be acquainted with the life and character of each, and to give to individuals from the common offerings of the faithful whatever would suffice for them to live properly and devoutly."[39] In his commentary on Ephesians, Bucer wrote that "Deacons are joined to the ministry of bishops and presbyters to minister to them and especially to care for the poor" and also that the office of deacons is "for the sustaining of the poor."[40] The role of the deacons in poor relief was significant—and pastoral. Bucer urged that "at certain times they should visit them or summon them in order to learn more precisely how they are enjoying the alms of the faithful, and what things they may be in need of at any given time."[41] Administratively, the deacons

> should keep an account of whatever comes to the churches for the use of the poor, either from the proceeds of property or the offerings of the faithful, and from this give to each of the poor whatever shall be found to be necessary for them to live to the Lord. And they must keep a faithful record of this in a book of expenses; for they should render an account of all receipts and expenditures . . . to the presbytery.[42]

39. Bucer, *De Regno Christi*, 256–57.

40. Cited in Hall, *Service in Christ*, 98. Bucer's views were highly influential in John Calvin's views on the nature of the office of deacons. See McKee, *John Calvin on the Diaconate*, 153–57.

41. Bucer, *De Regno Christi*, 308.

42. Bucer, *De Regno Christi*, 308–9.

"On this account," Bucer continued, "the Holy Spirit requires also of deacons that they be men approved, with a good reputation among the people of Christ (Acts 6:3)."[43]

Ministry in Church and Society

Bucer's structuring of the church's offices were reforming efforts. All was in the service of Jesus Christ, the Lord of the church. But Bucer's goals went further. As Greschat puts it: "His goal was continually the comprehensive renewal and Christian transformation of the whole of society—the church community as much as the civic commune, in other words, the respective spiritual and secular realms."[44] This meant all institutions and communities are subject to the Lordship of Christ. Communities can only flourish when their people serve God and obey God's commandments. If they do not, judgment and punishments will follow.

These perspectives gave impetus to a widespread embodiment of Bucer's emphasis—in *That No One Should Live for Himself but for Others*—that love of neighbor is basic to the whole of society. Society needed structures to hold and stabilize people—who are sinners—and to reorder societal structures toward their divine purposes. In his work *The Kingdom of Christ*, written for the young English king, Edward VI, Bucer set forth a program of reform that "advocates the reformation of religion not only in the context of worship and the Church but also relates it to the whole common life."[45] Bucer was concern that people live "well and happily" and also that societal structures be put in place to administer and manage so this purpose could be realized.

43. Bucer, *De Regno Christi*, 309.

44. Greschat, "The Relation between Church and Civil Community in Bucer's Reforming Work," 24.

45. Pauck in *Melanchthon and Bucer*, 163.

The church and the political government are both designed for this administration and management. Church and state exist in relation to the kingdom of Christ. As Pauck notes, this meant for Bucer that "under Christ, the Church and the State are responsible for the cultivation of true religion. Both must carry out his will."[46] Citizens must follow the law as "the dictates and prescriptions of God."[47] Bucer believed "the restitution of the Kingdom of Christ" could come only as the king sought to procure and preserve "justice, peace, and the well-being of his subjects."[48]

Ministry in church and society, for Bucer, would take the form of beginning with the clear and powerful Word of God so the church and the government could enact laws in which "all self-love and all greed be suppressed and that everyone embrace and help his neighbors and transact all things with them in the same good faith that everyone wishes other to have in entering into and making contracts with himself."[49] In this way, both church and society seek "the full restoration and renewal of the Kingdom of Christ."[50]

46. Pauck in *Melanchthon and Bucer*, 167. As Torrance explains: "The relations of the Church and State are mutual. The Word of God is communicated to the State through the Church, and in obedience to that Word the State creates within the world a sphere of liberty, setting bounds to the kingdom of Satan, so that the life of the Church protected by the State may freely grow in obedience to God's Word and in the exercise of love, and so assume the character of a Respublica or Societas Christiana," Torrance, *Kingdom and Church*, 87.

47. Bucer, *De Regno Christi*, 358.

48. Bucer, *De Regno Christi*, 358.

49. Bucer, *De Regno Christi*, 361.

50. Bucer, *De Regno Christi*, 388. As Amos put it: "While Bucer argues that the church and the state are distinct, he also argues that they must act in concert," with "mutual submission," a joint activity that is fundamental for "the full manifestation of Christ's kingdom in this world." The aim is that the rule of Christ is promoted in such a way that "church and society become two ways of speaking of the

QUESTIONS FOR DISCUSSION

1. Why was it important for Bucer to have a vigorous doctrine of the church?

2. Where do you see the marks of the church in the church's life today?

3. Why is it important for the church to have an "ordered ministry" with various church offices?

4. What are the strengths of stressing the church's ministry of love?

same reality." "The corpus Christi, the body of Christ as the body of believers, becomes the corpus Christianum, the Christian society, where the ecclesiastical and spiritual on the one hand and the secular and political on the other are combined into one under the rule of Christ." See Amos, "Martin Bucer's *Kingdom of Christ*," 199.

8

WORD AND SACRAMENTS

In a previous chapter (chapter 2) Bucer's understanding of Scripture was the focus. In the present chapter our focus will be the *preached* Word. That is, the Word spoken, and the Word enacted in the "Sacraments." Our aim, in short, will be to investigate and explicate Bucer's theology of preaching and his theology of the Sacraments.

Moving forward in our examination of Bucer and the Sacraments, we will have to remind ourselves that the topic at hand could fill several monographs and our treatment will scarcely scratch the surface of this central topic.

BUCER AND THE WORD SPOKEN

Martin Bucer was a preacher. He spent many years of his life preaching and teaching the Word of God. His understanding of that task was formed in part by the influence of Erasmus and in part by the influence of Luther and in part by the humanism then sweeping into the souls of Western Europe's intellectual elite. More precisely, Bucer saw his task as preacher to be that of explaining and applying the Word of God to his congregation in a way that was both faithful to the original meaning of the text and that was faithful to meeting the needs of the people. Bucer's preaching was exegetically informed and intentionally aimed at application. In this way, Bucer was one of the early "Reformed" pastors who focused on exegesis and application. A sort of preaching that has endured to the present in Reformed churches.

When did Bucer make this his lifelong method? Very early it seems. In fact, as early as 1520, according to N. Scott Amos. He writes:

> The earliest concrete evidence of Bucer's sympathies with the biblical humanist emphasis on Scripture in his own practice of teaching theology is found in 1520 while still in the Dominican convent at Heidelberg, when he began lecturing on the Psalms (rather than lecturing on Lombard's Sentences) in his capacity as sententarius.[1]

Bucer was a humanist who utilized humanist methodologies to read and interpret Scripture so that his preaching of the Word was methodologically humanistic and not scholastic. This turning from scholasticism and its Aristotelian philosophical base was a watershed moment in the history of European Christianity. Now, rather than philosophy being the "driving force" of interpretation and preaching, Scripture itself became the driver and the determinative. Bucer used the tools and methods of biblical humanists who wanted to interpret Scripture in light of its historical contexts and to emphasize Scripture's practical message for Christian living. This meant a turn away from abstract and speculative philosophical questions and focusing on

---

1. Amos, *Bucer, Ephesians*, 87.

biblical exegesis and interpretation. This is the approach that marked Bucer's method in his biblical commentaries.

Here are some examples of Bucer's preaching/teaching drawn from his lectures on Ephesians, so that readers hear him in his own words (in translation, to be fair) and thereby get a sense of how he worked. "[Paul] . . . wrote it as (so to speak) a most perfect commentary on the entire doctrine of Christ in which might be contained everything he had ever taught the Ephesians or others."[2] In Bucer's mind Paul wrote Ephesians as a compendium of Christian doctrine. A sort of brief systematic theology. And in interpreted Ephesians in that light. Furthermore: "Who, having once diligently and religiously read through this letter, may not see how rich it is with the doctrine of Christ, with the doctrine of eternal salvation, so that it teaches and explains all the principal topics [loci] of our religion, yes with few words, but with [words] incredibly clear, eloquent, full, and far from all obscurity?"[3]

Bucer did not interpret Ephesians as a mere occasional letter as it is customarily interpreted today, he interpreted it as a work of dogmatics. Bucer thought dogmatically and as a consequence he saw dogmatic material in many places.

Yet, for Bucer, dogmatics was not the purview of the theologians alone. It was also the spiritual food of the people of God on the whole. Amos observes: "Bucer was keen to attack the claim that the Scriptures are too difficult for the people of God to understand, put forth by those who [now quoting Bucer] 'dare to contend that the Divine Scriptures are so obscure, so ambiguous, that their certain and salutary sense must be derived not from [the Scriptures]

2. Amos, *Bucer, Ephesians*, 92.

3. Amos, *Bucer, Ephesians*, 93.

themselves but only from the commentaries of the Holy Fathers and from the authority of the Church.'"[4]

Bucer the exegete was Bucer the theologian. Bucer the theologian was Bucer the exegete. The two were, in him, inseparable. But Bucer was not chiefly known among his contemporaries as an exegete. He was known among them as the man who sought harmony between the various factions of anti-Roman Catholic Christians of Europe. Bucer was known primarily, in his own time as in subsequent times, as the man who tried his best to persuade non-Roman Christians to agree on the meaning of the Eucharist. Accordingly, it is to Bucer as interpreter of the Sacraments that we now turn.

BUCER ON BAPTISM

Aside from the Anabaptists who first arose in 1525 in Zurich, European Christians, both Protestant, Reformed, and Catholic, agreed that baptism was sacramental and should be administered to children as a means by which to eliminate the stain of original sin and prepare the child for life in the Christian community. But what did Bucer and other Reformed theologians believe of the Sacraments in general? The Second Helvetic Confession states it precisely:

> The sacraments of the new people are Baptism and the Lord's Supper. There are some who count seven sacraments of the new people. Of these we acknowledge that repentance, the ordination of ministers (not indeed the papal but apostolic ordination), and matrimony are profitable ordinances of God, but not sacraments. Confirmation and extreme unction are human inventions which the Church can dispense with without any loss, and indeed, we do not have

4. Amos, *Bucer, Ephesians*, 97.

them in our churches. For they contain some things of which we can by no means approve.[5]

Infant baptism was practiced by Bucer and believed by Bucer to be the proper and good means of administration. He was, in sum, not a Baptist.

Bucer spells out his own understanding of baptism in the Tetrapolitan Confession. There he writes, in full (since the whole is relevant and important, the whole is here reproduced):

> Of Baptism, therefore, we confess that which Scripture in various places declares of it: that by it we are buried into Christ's death, are united into one body and put on Christ; that it is the washing of regeneration, that it washes away sins and saves us. All this we understand as St. Peter has interpreted when he says: "The like figure whereunto even baptism doth also now save us, not the putting away of the filth of the flesh, but the answer of a good conscience toward God." For without faith it is impossible to please God, and we are saved by grace, not by our works. But since Baptism is the sacrament of the covenant that God makes with those who are his, promising to be their God and Protector, as well as of their seed, and to have them as his people, and finally, since it is a symbol of renewing through the Spirit, which occurs through Christ, our theologians teach that it is to be given infants also, no less than formerly under Moses they were circumcised. For we are indeed the children of Abraham. Therefore no less to us than to those of old pertains the promise: I will be thy God and the God of thy seed.[6]

5. Second Helvetic Confession, chapter 19.

6. Tetrapolitan Confession, chapter 17.

Very few Reformed would quibble with this assertion. Even today, most Reformed Christians have adopted the same understanding of the sacrament of baptism. The benefit of Bucer's statement is that it is so precise and eloquent.

More's the pity, then, that the same agreement could not be reached in the matter of the Lord's Supper. For there, on that doctrine, and on it alone, Reformed and Lutheran and Catholic parted ways in a decisive and consequential manner.

BUCER ON THE MASS

As early as 1524 Bucer was writing about his understanding of the Mass. In a little booklet published that year, "*Grund und Ursach,*" Bucer would observe

> For since light has nothing in common with darkness, Christ no relationship with Belial and the believer no share with the unbeliever . . . we have, on the basis of Scripture, completely abolished and suppressed everything in our community which was added to the Lord's Supper to strengthen and embellish the contempt and mockery of Christ and of divine mercy. Thus we no more use the name "Mass," but instead "the Lord's Supper."[7]

That, in sum, is the attitude of Bucer on the ancient practice of the Mass. He viewed the Mass as the accretion of human traditions on top of the venerable and ancient practice of the Last Supper. The Supper was itself a beautiful Sacrament which communicated the goodness and mercy of Christ to those who participated in it. Hence, his abandonment of the very notion of the Mass, his insistence that Christians now simply call it by its biblical name, the Lord's

7. Thompson, *Eucharistic Sacrifice*, 99.

Supper, and that they strip away the layers of unnecessary human tradition.

BUCER ON THE LORD'S SUPPER

Regarding the Lord's Supper it's important to note that Catholics and Lutherans shared a basic understanding of the presence of Christ (Christ was really present bodily in the elements of the Supper) while Zwinglians held a view that was doubtful of the physical presence of Christ in the elements and instead saw his presence as symbolic, and the Supper itself as a memorial. Calvinists were generally somewhere between the Lutherans and the Zwinglians. Though this is a simplification of a very complex question, it does give the reader a sense of the basic notions held by the various theologians and their schools.

The fact that Bucer is best known for his attempt to facilitate agreement between the Lutherans and the Reformed (the Zwinglians) hardly needs to be mentioned. Indeed, it may be one of the few things people tend to know about Bucer. He wrote extensively on the subject and participated in the Marburg Colloquy held in 1529 in Marburg between Luther and Zwingli, Melanchthon, and Oecolampadius, and several others.

The participants at Marburg were able to agree on fourteen of fifteen points but regrettably they were unable to come to a common understanding of the Lord's Supper. And since that key issue was the very reason the colloquy was held, it is fair to say that the effort failed. Here is the article on the Lord's Supper, which both the Lutherans and the Zwinglians interpreted in their own favor:

> Fifteenth, regarding the Last Supper of our dear
> Lord Jesus Christ, we believe and hold that one
> should practice the use of both species [i.e., the

people receiving both the bread and the wine] as Christ himself did, and that the sacrament at the altar is a sacrament of the true body and blood of Jesus Christ and the spiritual enjoyment of this very body and blood is proper and necessary for every Christian. Furthermore, that the practice of the sacrament is given and ordered by God the Almighty like the Word, so that our weak conscience might be moved to faith through the Holy Spirit. And although we have not been able to agree at this time, whether the true body and blood of Christ are corporally present in the bread and wine [of Communion], each party should display towards the other Christian love, as far as each respective conscience allows, and both should persistently ask God the Almighty for guidance so that through his Spirit he might bring us to a proper understanding. Amen.[8]

The two sides agreed that congregants should receive both the bread and the wine, a practice that was not observed by Catholics. And that was where the agreement ended, for on every other point they adopted their own interpretations. Bucer himself stood somewhere in the middle, hovering towards the Zwinglian view.

Bucer's own interpretation of the Supper was stated in the Tetrapolitan Confession.[9] Composed in 1530, for the Diet of Augsburg, the Confession was an attempt to show the Emperor Charles V that the Reformed were indeed orthodox Christians in faith and practice (in spite of the Lutherans portrayal that they were other). There Bucer wrote:

8. *The Marburg Articles*, accessed on March 8, 2022. https://ghdi.ghi-dc.org/docpage.cfm?docpage_id=5245

9. With apologies for the extensive citations following, but they are critically important for a proper understanding of Bucer's views. On the Confession, see chapter 1.

> Concerning this venerable sacrament of the body and blood of Christ, all that the evangelists, Paul and the holy fathers, have left in writing, our men, in the best faith, teach, commend and inculcate. And hence with singular zeal they always publish this goodness of Christ to his people, whereby no less today than at that last Supper, to all those who sincerely have given their names among his disciples and receive this Supper according to his institution, he deigns to give his true body and true blood to be truly eaten and drunk for the food and drink of souls, for their nourishment unto life eternal.

His words are very carefully chosen. First, he asserts that the Reformed view of the sacrament of the Lord's Supper harkens back to Paul himself. Second, he notes that the Supper is only properly received by those who belong to Christ. Third, he calls the elements the "true" body and "true" blood of Jesus, which nonetheless are "food for souls," i.e., *spiritual* food. The elements, in other words, are spiritually consumed because they are spiritual themselves. In this regard, then, Bucer is Zwinglian. Though not what we might call a hard-core Zwinglian. Indeed, he continues

> Now, our ecclesiastics with especial diligence withdraw the minds of our people both from all contention and from all superfluous and curious inquiry to that which is alone profitable, and which was alone regarded by Christ our Saviour—namely, that, fed upon him, we may live in and through him a life pleasing to God, holy, and therefore eternal and blessed, and that we who partake of one bread in the Holy Supper may be among ourselves one bread and one body.

Bucer here shows himself unwilling to break fellowship with Christians of differing viewpoints. We may not know exactly how the Supper works as a sacrament, but we know it's true and we strive to get along with all those who also know that the Supper is meaningful and we refuse to disfellowship them simply because they see things differently than we do.

This is an extremely important point and one of the facts about Bucer that is most significant. Bucer strives for conciliation at every point, even the most contentious. His remark is utterly astounding and one that neither Luther nor Zwingli would ever make. Nor, it's fair to say, would Calvin or Bullinger. Bucer wants all Christians to be "one bread and one body." The other reformers would have liked it if every Christian accepted their interpretation of the Supper. Otherwise, unity was to them not as important as being right.

Bucer also pushes back against the Lutheran assertion that the Reformed are unorthodox in their view of the Supper. He writes

> From these things, which are truly in this manner, Thy Most Worshipful Majesty, Most Clement Emperor, doth know how falsely our adversaries proclaim that our men change Christ's words and do them violence by human glosses; that nothing save mere bread and mere wine is administered in our Supper; and thus that among us the Lord's Supper has been despised and rejected.

"Mere bread and mere wine" were how the Lutherans characterized the Reformed (Zwinglian) understanding of the Supper. This, Bucer insists, is simply false. The elements of the Supper are more than mere things and mere symbols. How they are more is part of the mystery of the incarnation but that they are not "mere flesh and blood" must also be understood. Here Bucer wishes to thread a middle way between Zwingli and Luther. He is showing that his, and the Reformed, understanding of the Supper is quite nuanced and not rightly or fairly boiled down to some slogan heaped on it by the adversaries of Zwingli.

Bucer concludes his statement on the Supper thusly:

> For with the greatest earnestness our men always teach and exhort that every man with simple faith embrace these words of the Lord, rejecting all devices and false glosses of men, and removing all wavering, apply his mind to their true meaning, and finally, with as great devotion as possible, receive these sacraments for the quickening nourishment of their souls and the grateful remembrance of so great a benefit; as is generally done now among us more frequently and devoutly than heretofore

Bucer pleads with the Emperor to understand that the Reformed teach their congregants the true faith and that means teaching them to accept the mystery of the Supper in faith, for the feeding of their souls and the enjoyment of their benefit.

Bucer's view of the Supper, then, is very similar to Zwingli's, though less combative and pugnacious than that of the hard-core Zwinglians. Bucer was willing to accept as Christians those who held differing views and he wished that he and those who believed as he did would also be accepted as Christian brothers and sisters.

Tragically, Bucer's goal was not achieved. The Reformed did not accept the Lutherans and the Lutherans did not accept the Reformed. Bucer, in short, sadly, failed. Both at Marburg and more largely in his many attempts to bring harmony to the non-Catholic Christians of Europe.

BUCER'S FAILURE

On January 22, 1531 Luther wrote to Bucer

> I have become so much aware of this that I am convinced that all the gates of hell, the whole papacy, all of Turkey, the whole world, all the flesh, and whatever evils there are could not have harmed the gospel at all, if we had only been of one mind. But what am I to do with something which cannot be accomplished? If you wish to be fair, then you will attribute the fact that I shun this unity not to stubbornness, but to the urging of my conscience and to the force of my faith.[10]

Luther would not bend. He would not change his view. Even for the sake of the gospel. In his mind, doing so would violate his own faith and his own conscience. Very importantly, though, even Melanchthon was predisposed to the view of Bucer!

> Melanchthon rejects the idea that "the bread is substantially the body of Christ," as well as that "the bread is the true body of Christ." Instead, he claims that the bread is "united with" (*consociatio cum*) the body of Christ, and only "in the use" and "not without cognition," not in such a way that it could be eaten by mice. He rejects the idea that the body is "in the bread or in the species of the bread, as if the true sacrament was instituted for the sake of the bread and the Papist adoration."[11]

Bucer's failure can be laid not so much at the feet of Bucer as at the feet of Luther. And also those of Zwingli, who would also not bend. Bucer attempted to find a path

10. *Luther's Works*, Vol 50, Letter 238.

11. Hovda, *The Controversy over the Lord's Supper*, 50–51.

for unity but that path was blocked by the Himalaya of Luther and the Atlantic of Zwingli.

And yet what history remembers is that Bucer failed. And Bucer himself long lamented the fact that he was unable to bring the two sides together. As early as 1533 Bucer expresses his dismay regarding the failure (and his own part in that failure) of the two sides to come together at Marburg in a very long letter to Philip of Hesse. Written on July 11, Bucer notes that the Luther camp and the Zwingli camp were irreconcilable. And the fact that Luther insisted that he was right and everyone else was wrong simply hardened positions, stirred anger, and made reconciliation impossible.[12] Bucer's attempts failing, he would spend the remainder of his life trying to effect the reconciliation he so desperately wanted so that the gospel could be preached in one harmonious voice.

QUESTIONS FOR DISCUSSION

1. If you had to summarize Bucer's understanding of baptism, what would you say?

2. Why do you think it was so important to Bucer to bring Luther and Zwingli together?

3. Why do you think Bucer failed to reconcile the non-Catholic camps?

4. How do you see the significance of the sacramental debates playing out in the history of the church?

12. *Martin Bucer Briefwechsel*, Bd 10, 23.

9

THE STATE AND LAST THINGS

WHEN PETER STEPHENS WROTE that Bucer's work was as tightly connected to the city council of Strasbourg as Luther's to the elector of Saxony,[1] he was writing a statement that is not only true, but completely salutary for any investigation of Bucer's view of the magistracy, i.e., in our terminology, the state. Without the support of the magistrates, Bucer's reformatory efforts can no more be conceived than can Luther's or Calvin's or Zwingli's or Bullinger's or those of Oecolampadius. The church needed the state, just as much, if not more, than the state needed the church in sixteenth-century Europe.

To be sure, the relationship of state and church was not always rosy. One need only recall the expulsion of Calvin from Geneva in 1538 (before being asked to come back in 1541) or the decision of the city of Strasbourg to ask the

1. Stephens, *The Holy Spirit*, 167.

magistrates to suspend Bucer. Or, in the precise wording of Thomas Dandelet:

> In April of 1549, Martin Bucer, dejected leader of the Reformation in Strasbourg, left that city for England. After more than 25 years of service as a teacher, theologian and preacher, Bucer was suspended from his duties by the city Senate because he refused to accept their decision to abide by the conditions of the peace interim imposed by the Holy Roman emperor Charles V on the city in 1547. The interim restored various privileges and properties to the Catholics of Strasbourg, including the right to celebrate the mass, and Bucer refused to compromise with a power that he considered to be siding with the anti-Christ in Rome.[2]

Our examination of Martin Bucer's theology of the state, and later, the last things (eschatology), is based on the very simple fact that the magistrates' support of Bucer's actions was absolutely indispensable. Were it not for the government functionaries and their oversight of the cities in which Reformations happened, Bucer and his colleagues would never have been able to manage their break from Roman domination. To be sure, the state forced the church to move in directions it did not wish at several junctures; but, at least in the case of Zwingli, the church also forced the hands of the magistrates (in the disastrous Second Kappel War). Nevertheless, the church used the state just as the state used the church. We can now, with those basic facts in mind, turn fully to a consideration of Bucer's theology of the state.

---

2. Dandelet, *Politics and Reformations*, 539.

THE STATE

That Martin Bucer was heavily engaged with the government can be proven very simply from a sampling of his correspondence for just a few months in 1533.[3] During those months Bucer corresponded with the city of Constance thirty-eight times, Augsburg sixteen times, Basel eleven times, Zurich eight times, St Gallen seven times, Bern three times, Paris three times, Ulm three times, Wittenberg two times, and Orbe two times. That's a total of ninety-three letters between Bucer and government figures in six months. Over the entire span of his ministry there are hundreds and hundreds of exchanges between Bucer and the officials of cities across Europe.

Extensive engagement is one thing but it doesn't tell us how he understood the state from the perspective of theology. For that, we have to turn to his writings. And as has been the case in a number of instances, The Tetrapolitan Confession serves as a very useful, very concise, and very precise source to examine. In Bucer's theology "to exercise the office of magistrate is the most sacred function that can be divinely given."[4] It may seem, at first blush, that the office of the magistrate's description as the "most sacred" office is overblown. But Bucer's point will shortly be made.

THE STATE IN THE TETRAPOLITAN CONFESSION

Bucer commences as follows:

> For when they discharge their duty aright and in
> order the people prosper both in doctrine and in
> life, because God is wont so to control our affairs

3. Details here are drawn from *Bucer Briefwechsel*, Bd X, x.

4. The Tetrapolitan Confession, chapter XXIII, all translations are our own.

that in great part both the welfare and the destruction of subjects depend upon those who are governors. Therefore none exercise the duties of magistrate more worthily than they who of all are the most Christian and holy.

The correct discharge of the magistrate's office results in the dissemination of proper doctrine, which, naturally, is necessary for people to live rightly. And the magistrates who see to it that doctrine is rightly disseminated are Christian magistrates. Thus, in short, the ideal magistrate is the Christian magistrate, the man who is himself a devoted follower of Christ. These are the sorts of magistrates that Bucer envisions as working and exercising authority across the lands. Where Christians serve the Lord in governance, they are, indeed, the holders of the highest office because they ensure that the ministry of the Word operates unhindered, and proper doctrine is thereby set free to change the hearts and minds of citizens.

Holy Christians serving the Lord and thereby enabling the church's servants of the Lord to carry out their tasks is how Bucer imagines the magistracy to function properly. But Bucer goes a step further, asserting that "beyond all doubt, it happened that bishops and other ecclesiastical men were formerly promoted by most godly emperors and kings to the external government of affairs."

That is, in former days clerics were elevated to the magistracy and thus they operated the government as though it were an extension of the church itself. With this vision in mind, it is easy to see where Bucer is headed in terms of the function of the state: it is an extension, an arm, of the church, and society is a theocracy, though he does admit that there have been problems with this ideal, and it has not been realized in practice. He writes:

> In this matter, although they were religious and
> wise, there was this one fault—viz., that they
> were not able to render what was needful for the
> proper administration of both offices, and they
> had to fail, either in their duty to the churches
> in ruling them by the Word, or to the state in
> governing it with authority.

Very intriguingly Bucer here admits that a person attempting to serve the interests of the state will always fail to fully serve the church; and the person attempting to serve the interests of the church will always fail to fully serve the state. This insight may be one of Bucer's most important concerning the relationship of the state to the church and the Christian to both. His recognition that servants of the state serve the state primarily and that servants of the church serve the church primarily is one that is very much needed today, in a time when some appear to believe that serving the state is serving the church, and vice versa, and the lines between the two have been so broadly blurred.

The ideal that Bucer wished for could not be realized, as much as he desired it. And he knew it.

How did Bucer understand the state in other texts he composed? Did his views change? Or did he hold the same view of the state throughout his extensive ministry? To that question we now turn.

THE STATE IN THE FIRST HELVETIC CONFESSION[5]

Composed in 1536, the First Helvetic Confession expresses the thought of Bucer and the Swiss theologians involved in the project on the subject of the state in its 26th Article. In a few simple paragraphs the government is described as

5. Schaff, *Creeds*, Vol. 3, 211f.

deriving its power from God alone and serves to "protect and promote the true honor of God and right worship."[6] Indeed, it is tasked by God to "punish and eradicate all blasphemy" and carry out "what the ministers of the Church teach and expound from the Word of God."

Furthermore, "The government should govern the people according to just, divine laws, maintain general peace and prosperity, protect the public benefit, and punish anyone who transgresses these things." If the magistrates and officials do these things, then "They serve God her Lord as she is required to do."

For the citizen:

> We should all be obedient and aware of the State's supremacy, though we remain free in Christ, with our bodies, belongings, and property, and with love from the heart out of faith prove our subjection to it, take and keep oaths regarding it, so long as the State's biddings and commandments are not in opposition to Him for whose sake we honor and obey her.

Clearly, then, Bucer's views of the state were fairly consistent over time. He was convinced that the state existed to serve God. It did so by implementing the Word of God as explained and preached by the church's ministers. It rewarded well-doers and punished evil-doers. It lifted the poor in accordance with Scripture and it educated the young in terms of God and served its divine Master, just as did the church.

In short, Bucer would have wholly agreed with Luther, when he wrote: "The secular State is a divine ordinance which every person is obligated to obey and honor"[7] be-

6. Translations throughout of the German text are our own.

7. Luther, *WA* XXXI, 190.

cause it is divinely ordered and ordained. And again, Bucer would agree with Luther's comment that "If a judge functions in his office and condemns an evildoer to death, it is not his work, but God's task and work which he fulfills."[8]

When Martin Bucer looked at the state, he saw the finger of God. He saw God at work in the world—when, that is, the state worked in support of the gospel. But states are not perfect and their servants are not perfect, so no matter how much Christians might pine for better, they would live in complete disappointment if they had no hope to look forward to in the divine future. It is to the eternal denouement, then, that we now must turn our attention.

Last Things

Briefly put, "eschatology" refers to the theological doctrine of the "last things": death, judgment, heaven, and hell; it thus concerns "the ultimate fate of all created beings and things."[9] Regrettably, Bucer penned no commentary on the Book of Revelation and he left behind no systematic treatment of the doctrine of eschatology. He doesn't discuss it in the First Helvetic Confession and he doesn't in the Tetrapolitan Confession. We can only glean bits and pieces of his eschatology here and there as his notions on the topic are never treated systematically.

Another fragment can be found in Bucer's mention of hell in his lengthily titled "*In Sacra Qvatvor Euangelia, Enarrationes perpetuae: Quibus inspersi sunt syncerioris Theologiae Loci communes, ad Scripturarum fidem simpliciter & nullius cum insectatione tractati: adiectis etiam aliquot locorum tractationibus, & Indice copiosissimo*" (Stephanus,

8. Luther, *WA* XXXII, 324.

9. Barnes, *Companion to Reformation Theology*, 233.

1553).[10] There Bucer observes simply that those sentenced to hell will suffer the torments there forever.

Bucer is far more concerned with this life than the next and it seems very clear that his view of eternity, the afterlife, or heaven and hell was traditionalist and "standard." What's very interesting in this connection is the fact that neither Luther nor Zwingli ever made any extensive description of their understanding of the afterlife. To be sure, the argument from silence is not proof, but their silence, and Bucer's, on the topic, speaks, it seems to us, volumes.

The reason for the apparent silence of Bucer and others of the early Reformation is that the issue really didn't become pressing until later, with the second generation Lutheran and Reformed theologians. Gerhard Sauter writes:

> The term "eschatology" (*eschatologia*) stems from its use in Philipp Heinrich Friedlieb's *Dogmatics* (1644), followed by Abraham Calov in his voluminous *Systema locorum Theologicorum* (1655–77). Other Lutheran theologians, most prominently Johann Gerhard in his *Loci Theologici* (1610–22), compiled the doctrine of "the last things" entitled *De Novissimis* as the end piece of a general presentation of theology. Occasionally, the term "final things" (*extrema*) was used. These three terms mean the last, ultimate, and definite state of all created things in the face of eternity and the "other world," the world to come."[11]

---

10. *Continuous Narrative of the Holy Four Gospels: To Which the Common Places of a More Sincere Theology Were Sprinkled, Treated Simply, Being Faithful to the Scriptures and with None of the Annoyances: with the Addition Also of Several Treatises on Theological Themes, and a Very Copious Index.*

11. Sauter, *Oxford Handbook of Eschatology*, 348.

Nonetheless, it is possible to find threads of the doctrine as early as Calvin and his 1559 edition of the *Institutes of the Christian Religion*.

The Last Things in Calvin's Theology

Thus, when it comes to how reformers viewed the life after death, we are left with only John Calvin's writings. In order, therefore, to gain some perspective on Bucer's views we will look at the views of Calvin with the understanding that while Calvin's view may have been Bucer's in general, Bucer's may have been nuanced here and there in a direction not particularly Calvin-esque. As suggested above, we simply do not know Bucer's precise views on this matter since he never made a systematic presentation of them.

That said, how did a Christian theologian of the non-Catholic camp understand the afterlife in the middle and late sixteenth century? John Calvin will be our guide. He discusses three aspects of what we think of when we think of the last things: the afterlife (in general, *Inst.* III.9), the resurrection of the dead (*Inst.* III.25), and the eternal blessedness of the elect and misery of the damned (*Inst.* III.25.12).

THE AFTERLIFE IN GENERAL, *INST.* III.9

Calvin treats "The Future Life" in Book III, chapter 9 of his *Institutes.* What follows is drawn from that chapter.

Calvin begins his argument with a discussion of the present life and its many troubles, which, he asserts, is all allowed by God so that his people will crave the next life. Things like prosperity hinder people from desiring the future life and so God takes action to ameliorate that hindrance. Still, he argues, the present life is God's good gift and so it must be taken with all seriousness. It is only then, in *Inst. III.9.4* that Calvin actually takes time to describe the life to come, in comparison to the present life. He concludes the chapter with a summons for believers to be fearless in the face of death.

What this brief outline of Calvin's treatment of the afterlife shows is that he has almost as little interest in the particulars as Zwingli and Luther and Bucer. He writes:

> If heaven is our country, what can the earth be but a place of exile? If departure from the world is entrance into life, what is the world but a sepulchre, and what is residence in it but immersion in death? If to be freed from the body is to gain full possession of freedom, what is the body but a prison? If it is the very summit of happiness to enjoy the presence of God, is it not miserable to want it? But "whilst we are at home in the body, we are absent from the Lord," (2 Cor. 5:6). Thus when the earthly is compared with the heavenly life, it may undoubtedly be despised and trampled under foot. We ought never, indeed, to regard it with hatred, except in so far as it keeps us subject to sin; and even this hatred ought not to be directed against life itself. At all events, we must stand so affected towards it in regard to weariness or hatred as, while longing for its termination, to be ready at the Lord's will to continue in it, keeping far from everything like murmuring and impatience. For it is as if the Lord had assigned us a post, which we must maintain till he recalls us.[12]

It is indeed intriguing that, as Bucer, Calvin's primary concern seems to be the present life and how Christians can and should best make their way in it. To be sure, they need

12. Calvin, *Institutes*, III.9.4.

to have one eye on their future, but they also need to have one eye on the present. Indeed, they must "man their post" here in this life as long as God wills it. It is highly doubtful that Bucer would have disagreed with any of this. No such disagreement has yet been located by the present authors.

When Calvin turns to an examination of the resurrection of the dead he does so in III.25.

THE RESURRECTION OF THE DEAD (*INST.* III.25)

The hope of life after the present life, Calvin asserts, animates believers. It is unknown to philosophers and it is as certain as any other teaching of the Bible. There is, Calvin, and Bucer, asserted, life after death. Jesus was raised, bodily, physically, corporeally, and so will those be who belong to him. God, the assertion continues, is certainly capable of achieving this.

Calvin then spends a good bit of time putting the views of atheists and "Sadducees" and chiliasts and universalists and "Manichees" to rest. Afterwards, he shows that the godless too are raised, to everlasting destruction. Calvin writes:

> I have deferred the brief consideration to be given of it to this place, that my readers may learn, when they have received Christ, the author of perfect salvation, to rise higher, and know that he is clothed with heavenly immortality and glory in order that the whole body may be rendered conformable to the Head. For thus the Holy Spirit is ever setting before us in his person an example of the resurrection.[13]

That Jesus was truly raised, and that his people will be as well is a core truth that may not be disbelieved. Calvin

---

13. Calvin, *Institutes*, III.25.3.

again: "To refuse assent to these numerous and authentic proofs is not diffidence, but depraved and therefore infatuated obstinacy."[14]

For Calvin—as for, presumably, Bucer and Zwingli and Luther and Oecolampadius and Melanchthon—Jesus was really physically and bodily raised from the dead, and as a consequence so too will Christians be.

But what of the life to be experienced after the resurrection? What did Calvin and his contemporaries believe about the actual substance of life after death? What would it be like? What kind of state was it? To that final topic we now turn our attention.

THE ETERNAL BLESSEDNESS OF THE ELECT AND MISERY OF THE DAMNED (*INST.* III.25.12)

Calvin devotes the closing paragraph to the question of the kind of existence the elect will experience after their resurrection. In terms of the modern way of putting that question, he wonders "what it will be like in heaven for Christians." Once more we remind ourselves that, since there is no comparable description in Bucer's extant writings (yet discovered by the present writers) we must rely on Calvin as a representative of their common Reformed camp.

At this juncture, Calvin is characteristically hesitant to say what Scripture does not say. His hesitance is based on his belief that where Scripture is silent it is not wise to speculate. And Scripture is hauntingly silent on the topic at hand: nearly as silent as Bucer himself.

Most interestingly, the great bulk of the paragraph describes the absolute misery of the damned, about which

14. Calvin, *Institutes*, III.25.3.

Scripture has plenty to say. Near the end of his description of hell's horrors he writes

> Hence unhappy consciences find no rest, but are vexed and driven about by a dire whirlwind, feeling as if torn by an angry God, pierced through with deadly darts, terrified by his thunderbolts and crushed by the weight of his hand; so that it were easier to plunge into abysses and whirlpools than endure these terrors for a moment. How fearful, then, must it be to be thus beset throughout eternity![15]

Of the blessed he writes:

> there will be so much pleasantness in the very sight [of heaven], so much delight in the very knowledge, that this happiness will far surpass all the means of enjoyment which are now afforded. Let us suppose ourselves placed in the richest quarter of the globe, where no kind of pleasure is wanting, who is there that is not ever and anon hindered and excluded by disease from enjoying the gifts of God? who does not oftentimes interrupt the course of enjoyment by intemperance? Hence it follows, that fruition, pure and free from all defect, though it be of no use to a corruptible life, is the summit of happiness.[16]

In the hereafter the damned will suffer immeasurable misery and conversely the blessed will enjoy immeasurable happiness. More than that, and any description of the particular delights of heaven are left unsaid by Calvin. And they are certainly left unsaid by Bucer.

15. Calvin, *Institutes*, III.25.12.
16. Calvin, *Institutes*, III.25.11.

CONCLUSION

An examination of Martin Bucer's understanding of the state is not as disconnected from his views of the last things as one might initially imagine. The state has to do with life in this world and how Christians are to live in the here and now. The last things have to do with life after this one and since Scripture says very little of it, except regarding the misery of the damned, then the focus of the Christian should be on life in this world, life lived in obedience to God.

Uniting in one discussion Bucer's view of life in this world and life in the next; and our discovery that he has very little to say of the latter, simply reinforces our earlier observations that Bucer wants above all else for Christians to live as the disciples of the Crucified and Risen Lord in the here and now. That life should be characterized by a desire to be obedient to their Lord and united in their efforts to share the gospel with the world. If Christians are too keen to escape this life, they will be of little use to it. But if they have one eye on this life and one on the next, they will live balanced, productive, godly lives and thus will communicate the gospel in deed as well as in word. And that, in Bucer's mind, is the aim of the Christian life.

Christians are citizens of the next world, but they are also pilgrim citizens of this world. They are obliged to both. That is how Bucer understood earth and heaven:

> Now, we know that a kingdom, if it is rightly and properly so called, is said to be the administration of a people or state by which the one person who excels the others in wisdom and every virtue so arranges and obtains whatever is for the well-being of the citizens that nothing at all is lacking to them, in such a way that from earliest

childhood everyone is formed and led toward a responsible and happy way of life.[17]

Bucer would assert this of earthly kingdoms and he would also believe it of the heavenly kingdom.

QUESTIONS FOR DISCUSSION

1. How does Bucer's view of the state differ from Luther's?

2. If you had to summarize Bucer's theology of the government, what would you say?

3. Bucer's view of the state is both similar to and dissimilar from Calvin's. What are those similarities and what are those differences?

4. Why do you think Bucer had so little to say about the next life?

5. Do you think it's fair to see Calvin's view of the last things as a lens to understand Bucer?

6. How do you understand the doctrine of the last things?

17. Bucer, *De Regno Christi*, 177.

10

THE ABIDING SIGNIFICANCE OF MARTIN BUCER

MARTIN BUCER'S LIFE AND times may seem far removed from our own. They are, of course. Nonetheless, we can rightly ask, "What is the abiding or ongoing significance of Bucer's life and theology for today?" What insights and emphases in Bucer's thought can continue to be of key importance for Christian churches and Christian lives in our time?

Our presentation of Martin Bucer did not deal fully with all his many activities and ministries. He was one of the great Protestant theologians of the sixteenth century, well-respected by his colleagues. Bucer was a church reformer and leader who cared deeply about the whole body of Christian believers. He sought to organize the church and its ministries in ways that would be faithful to the Christian gospel and serve Jesus Christ.

We believe Martin Bucer speaks to us today with important convictions and directions that can bless Christian churches and deepen our lives of Christian faith. Here are Bucer's emphases and accents which we think are vital.

WORD AND SPIRIT ARE DYNAMIC

Bucer's life was focused on the Word of God. The Word of God comes to us supremely in Jesus Christ (John 1:1). Christ is made known to us by the Word of God in Holy Scripture. Scripture's message comes to us as the Word of God in preaching. This threefold Word of God formed a foundation of Bucer's life and ministry.

Martin Bucer was concerned always to interpret and understand God's Word in Scripture. His teachings about Christian doctrine were to be grounded in solid biblical understandings. "Concerning the things of God," said Bucer, "nothing is to be taught unless it is either expressly set out in the Scriptures, or may be truly and certainly proved from the same."[1] To that end, Bucer devoted his life to the interpretation of the Bible. His biblical commentaries and all his theological writings focused on how Holy Scripture is to be understood. Bucer used available resources to help him interpret the biblical message so it can be proclaimed to the church and the world.

But Bucer stressed that the Holy Spirit was the prime interpreter of the biblical message. The Spirit brings faith—and the personal faith that Jesus Christ is Lord and Savior as well as that Scripture is the Word of God. The Spirit guides us "into all the truth" (John 16:13), illuminating our understanding of what the Bible means for us.

Word and Spirit are inextricably bound up together for Bucer (and all Protestants). Word and Spirit are dynamic.

1. Bucer, *Common Places*, 78.

As one reads Scripture, the Spirit illumines the message of Scripture for us. Relatedly, when we think the Spirit is prompting us or moving into some decision or direction in life, we must check our understanding in relation to the teachings of the Bible. We pray for God's Spirit to illumine us to what God is saying in Scripture. We base our lives on Scripture as the source of what we believe and how we live.

Word and Spirit are dynamic. Through the Scriptures and the Spirit we live as disciples of Jesus Christ who seek to do God's will.

JESUS CHRIST IS CENTRAL

John 3:16 proclaims: "For God so loved the world that he gave his only Son, so that everyone who believes in him may not perish but may have eternal life." This is the central message of the Bible and for Bucer the Scriptures point us, always, to Jesus Christ. Jesus said, "The works that I do in my Father's name testify to me" (John 10:25). The whole of Scripture testifies to Jesus Christ who, said Bucer, "died for our sins, and rose again for our justification."[2]

Human sin needs forgiven. Through the death of Jesus Christ on the cross, God pardons human sin, overcoming the alienation of humans with their Creator, the one in whose image we are created. "There must be awakened in us by the operation of the Holy Spirit," wrote Bucer, "a heartfelt repentance and sorrow" for sin. "God takes pity on us" and "for the sake of his dear Son," Bucer said, God sends us "the holy gospel of his grace, of the redemption which his only Son, our Lord Jesus Christ, has won for us by his bitter suffering and death" while also giving us God's "Holy Spirit to bring us to a true, complete and sincere belief in

2. Bucer, *Common Places*, 78.

his gospel,"[3] Through faith in our Lord Jesus Christ, "we are justified before God from all our sins, accounted worthy of eternal life, and born anew as the children and heirs of God, without any merit of our works."[4]

This message of the Christian gospel is what the church proclaims. The central message is Jesus Christ himself in his person and work through which the elect of God, in Bucer's understanding, receive the gift of eternal life which was prepared for them "before the foundation of the world" (Eph 1:4). By the work of the Holy Spirit faith is given and "by means of that faith of the gospel by which they wholly and truly believe in our Lord Jesus Christ, an attitude of sincere trust in God as their Father . . . and in Christ our Lord as their only Savior. . . . This Spirit therefore also produces in all such a firm hope in all the grace and help of God, and in eternal life."[5]

Jesus Christ is central to all our beliefs and to our lives of faith.

THE CHURCH IS A COMMUNITY OF LOVE

"Through the Holy Spirit and true faith . . . all who have been born anew in Christ the Lord and possess justifying faith are members of the body of Christ, and live and abide in him," wrote Bucer.[6] Since God sent Jesus Christ as Savior out of divine love, the people of God drawn together by the Spirit into the church are to live that love which brings them together in the Spirit. The church is a community of love. This emphasis of Bucer remains a defining characteristic of the Christian church in our times and for our lives.

3. Bucer, *Common Places*, 79.

4. Bucer, *Common Places*, 79–80.

5. Bucer, *Common Places*, 79–80.

6. Bucer, *Common Places*, 82.

This unity of the Spirit, of which love is the primary mark, is the basis of the church's unity in Jesus Christ. For Bucer, the unity of the children of God is not found in doctrine by itself, but in the community's common life of faith and love. Bucer saw faith as issuing in a "confidence in God's kindness and hope of eternal life, accompanied by an all-consuming zeal for God and true worship of him, and hence also true love of our neighbour and earnest devotion to total righteousness and holiness."[7] Bucer agreed with Augustine that true faith is a "faith that works through love" (Gal 5:6). Bucer said, "Let no one be offended at his describing love of one's neighbour as the definition of faith, a definition in terms of the effect."[8] A song used to put it: "And they will know we are Christians by our love." Faith must express itself in loving others, or else it is not genuine faith. The Christian church—the faith community—is to be marked by its giving visible action to the reality of life, as an expression of faith.

Jesus said to his disciples that they are "to love one another" (John 13:34; 15:12), Bucer noted and "by this love we are recognized as being his disciples." "This love," wrote Bucer, is "the fulfilment of the law of God, in that by it a [person] is led to learn, do, suffer or avoid everything according as it will best promote the temporal and eternal welfare of his neighbour (Rom. 13.8ff.; Gal. 5.14; 2 Cor. 13.11; 1 Cor. 9:19–23)."[9] For Bucer, this meant the church should be active in relief of the poor and providing for human need, wherever it is found.

Churches today will continue to find ways to express love for others—in society and in the family of faith itself. "For faith shows its power through love," said Bucer, which

---

7. Bucer, *Common Places*, 195.

8. Bucer, *Common Places*, 195–96.

9. Bucer, *Common Places*, 80.

always manages to benefit [others], and to be injurious to no one (1 Cor. 13:5)."[10]

THE SACRAMENTS SHOULD UNITE

Since the sixteenth century, Protestant churches have recognized two sacraments: Baptism and the Lord's Supper.

Bucer said of sacraments that they are "visible words whereby in accordance with [God's] ordinance his favour and promises were formerly commended, precisely by virtue of being ordained by the Lord actually presented in their own fashion what they signified."[11] In the sacraments, God's promises are conveyed and are effective.

Bucer's theology of baptism included infant baptism. In the sixteenth century, groups emerged that rejected infant baptism as valid. They were called "Anabaptists" and believed only adult, "believer's baptism" was valid in the sight of God. In light of this conviction, Anabaptists left Lutheran and Reformed churches to establish churches where only "believer's baptism" was practiced. In this way, the sacrament of baptism did not unite Protestant churches, it split them.

One of the most contested, contentious, and divisive issues of the Reformation period was the theological understandings of the Lord's Supper; and more specifically if—and in what way—Jesus Christ is "present" in the Supper. This was the issue that prevented a unanimous agreement of Lutheran and Reformed leaders at the Colloquy of Marburg (1529), as discussed above. It has always seemed ironic that the Last Supper—the meal Jesus gave his disciples before his death—a meal that should have united them

10. Bucer, *De Regno Christi*, 196.

11. Bucer, *Common Places*, 293.

together in the love of Jesus became, for the later church, a source of strife and division.

This past in which sacraments have divided rather than united churches is what we have inherited. But Bucer worked long and hard trying to bring different theological understandings together and to give visible expression to the unity of the church. He was a theologian of dialogue, seeking to find common theological ground among various viewpoints, as possible. For Bucer, the unity of the church was a unity of the Spirit. He sought to take seriously Paul's injunction: "making every effort to maintain the unity of the Spirit in the bond of peace" (Eph 4:3). For Bucer, the church was united in "the unity of the Spirit, of love, the word of God, Christ, the sacraments, and the sharing of gifts, that we may aspire together to the same goal, and hold and express the same beliefs."[12]

Today, we should make all efforts possible to maintain the "unity of the Spirit in the bond of peace," including celebrating ways the church's sacraments can unite us, bring us together in the body of Christ, instead of driving us apart. Today we need to hear Bucer when he says: "It is essential that we hold completely in common everything instituted for the building up of the Church."[13]

ABIDING SIGNIFICANCE

Martin Bucer stands as a Protestant reformer who focused on the Christian gospel, which centered on Jesus Christ as God's eternal Son who died for human sin. The Holy Spirit brings the gift of faith to God's elect, unites them in the church. Scripture guides the people of God as they are nourished by Word and Sacrament. God's Spirit calls the

12. Bucer, *Common Places*, 208.

13. Bucer, *Common Places*, 208.

church to minister to the world by sharing the love of God in Jesus Christ. May we hear and obey the Spirit's call!

QUESTIONS FOR DISCUSSION

1. What ways are you conscious of being guided and nurtured by God's Word and Spirit, as Bucer taught?

2. What are important elements in Bucer's understanding of Jesus Christ that makes him central to Christian faith and life?

3. In what ways do you find contemporary churches expressing Bucer's emphasis on the church as a community of love? How relevant do you consider such an emphasis today?

4. What is important in Bucer's views of the Sacraments and in what ways are they of "abiding significance" for theology and Christians today?

5. How do you see Bucer's life-experiences as being formative for his theology?

SELECTED BIBLIOGRAPHY

PRIMARY SOURCES

Aquinas, Thomas. *Summa Theologica*. Rome: Ex Typographia Senatus, 1866.

Bucer, Martin. *Common Places of Martin Bucer*. Translated and edited by D. F. Wright. The Courtenay Library of Reformation Classics 4. Appleford, UK: Sutton Courtenay, 1972.

———. *Instruction in Love, by Martin Bucer, the Reformer*. Translated by Paul Traugott Fuhrmann. 1952. Reprint, Eugene, OR: Wipf & Stock, 2008.

———. *Martin Bucers Deutsche Schriften*. Edited by Robert Stupperich et al. Gutersloh: Gutersloher Verlagshaus, 1960–.

———. *Martini Buceri opera latina*. Edited by Hans Virck et al. Paris: Presses Universitaires de France, 1954–.

———. Primary sources available at the Post-Reformation Digital Library. Online: https://www.prdl.org/author_view.php?a_id=173.

———. *De Regno Christi* in *Melanchthon and Bucer*. Edited by Wilhelm Pauck. The Library of Christian Classics, Vol. 19. Philadelphia: Westminster, 1969.

Calvin, John. Primary sources available at the Post-Reformation Digital Library. Online: https://www.prdl.org/author_view.php?a_id=1.

Luther, Martin. *Luther's Works*, Vol. 50: Letters III. Edited by Jaroslav Jan Pelikan. Philadelphia: Fortress, 1999.

———. Primary sources available at the Post-Reformation Digital Library. Online: https://www.prdl.org/author_view.php?a_id=8, including the *Weimar Ausgabe* (WA, below).

Schaff, Philip. *The Creeds of Christendom with a History and Critical Notes.* 3 vols. New York: Harper & Brothers, 1882. Online: https://ccel.org/ccel/schaff/creeds1/creeds1.ix.ii.iv.html

SECONDARY SOURCES

Allen, Michael, and Scott R. Swain, eds. *The Oxford Handbook of Reformed Theology.* Oxford: Oxford University Press, 2020.

————. *Reformed Theology.* New York: T&T Clark, 2010.

Amos, N. Scott. *Bucer, Ephesians and Biblical Humanism: The Exegete as Theologian.* New York: Springer, 2015.

————. "Martin Bucer's *Kingdom of Christ.*" In *The Oxford Handbook of Reformed Theology*, edited by Michael Allen and Scott R. Swain, 189–202. Oxford: Oxford University Press, 2020.

Bagchi, David, and David C. Steinmetz, eds. *The Cambridge Companion to Reformation Theology.* New York: Cambridge University Press, 2004.

Barnes, Robin, ed. *T. & T. Clark Companion to Reformation Theology.* London: Bloomsbury T. & T. Clark, 2014.

Burnett, Amy Nelson. "Church Discipline and Moral Reformation in the Thought of Martin Bucer." *Sixteenth Century Journal* 22 (1991) 438–56.

Burnett, Amy Nelson. *The Yoke of Christ—Martin Bucer and Christian Discipline.* Kirksville, MO: Sixteenth Century Journal, 1994.

Cochrane, Arthur C. *Reformed Confessions of the 16th Century with a New Introduction by Jack Rogers.* Louisville, KY: Westminster John Knox, 2003.

De Boer, E. "Christology and Christianity: The Theological Power of the Threefold Office in Lord's Day 12." *Die Skriflig/In Luce Verbi* 47.2 (2013) 1–8.

De Kroon, Marijn. *Martin Bucer und Johannes Calvin. Reformatorische Perspektiven.* Einleitung und Texte. Vandenhoeck & Ruprecht, 1991.

De Kroon, Marijn, and Willem van't Spijker. *Martin Bucer (1491-1551): Collected Studies on His Life, Work, Doctrine, and Influence.* Edited by Christa Boerke and Jan C. Klok. Refo 500 Academic Studies, 44. Göttingen: Vandenhoeck & Ruprecht, 2018.

Eells, Hastings, *Martin Bucer.* New Haven, CT: Yale University Press, 1931.

Eire, Carlos. *War against the Idols: The Reformation of Worship from Erasmus to Calvin.* Cambridge: Cambridge University Press, 1986.

Greschat, Martin. *Martin Bucer: A Reformer and His Times.* Translated by Stephen E. Buckwalter. Louisville, KY: Westminster John Knox, 2004.

———. "The Relation between Church and Civil Community in Bucer's Reforming Work." In *Martin Bucer: Reforming Church and Community,* edited by D. F. Wright, 17–31. Cambridge: Cambridge University Press, 2002.

Harnack, Adolf von. *History of Dogma.* Reprint, Eugene, OR: Wipf and Stock, 1997.

Hovda, Bjørn Ole. *The Controversy over the Lord's Supper in Danzig 1561–1567.* Gottingen: Vandenhoeck and Ruprecht, 2017.

Köhler, Walther. *Das Marburger Religionsgespräch 1529. Versuch einer Rekonstruktion.* Leipzig, 1929.

Lang, Augustus. *Der Evangelienkommentar Martin Butzers und die Grundzüge.* Leipzig: Di-eterich'sche Verlags-Buchhandlung, 1900.

———. "Martin Bucer." *The Evangelical Quarterly* 1.2 (1929) 159–65.

Lugioyo, Brian. *Martin Bucer's Doctrine of Justification: Reformation Theology and Early Modern Irenicism.* Oxford Studies in Historical Theology. New York: Oxford University Press, 2010.

McCord, James I., and T. H. L. Parker. *Service in Christ: Essays Presented to Karl Barth on His 80th Birthday.* Grand Rapids: Eerdmans, 1966.

McKee, Elsie A. *John Calvin on the Diaconate and Liturgical Almsgiving.* Travaux d'Humanisme et Renaissance CXCVII. Genève: Librairie Droz, 1984.

Ocker, Christopher, Michael Printy, Peter Starenko, and Peter Wallace, eds. *Politics and Reformations: Polities, Nations, and Empires: Essays in Honor of Thomas A. Brady, Jr.* Leiden: Brill, 2007.

Pauck, Wilhelm. *Melanchthon and Bucer.* The Library of Christian Classics. Philadelphia: Westminster, 1969.

———. "The Ministry in the Time of the Continental Reformation." In *The Ministry in Historical Perspectives,* edited by H. Richard Niebuhr and Daniel D. Williams, chapter 5. New York: Harper and Row, 1983.

Rogers, Jack B., and Donald K. McKim. *The Authority and Interpretation of the Bible: An Historical Approach with a New Epilogue.* Reprint, Eugene, OR: Wipf & Stock, 1999.

Sinnema, Donald. "Doctrinal Dissension among Delegates at the Synod of Dordt (1618–1619)." In *A Landmark in Turbulent Times: The Meaning and Relevance of the Synod of Dordt (1618–1619)*, edited by Henk van den Belt er al., 173–91. Refo500 Academic Studies. Göttingen: Vanderhoeck & Ruprecht, 2022.

Steinmetz, David. *Reformers in the Wings: From Geiler von Kaysersberg to Theodore Beza*. 1971. Reprint, Oxford: Oxford University Press, 2001.

Stephens, W. Peter. "The Church in Bucer's Commentaries on the Epistle to the Ephesians." In *Martin Bucer: Reforming Church and Community*, edited by D. F. Wright, 45–60. Cambridge: Cambridge University Press, 2002.

———. *The Holy Spirit in the Theology of Martin Bucer*. New York: Cambridge University Press, 1970.

Stupperich, Robert. "Martin Bucer als Theologe und Kirchenmann." *Die Zeichen der Zeit* 5 (1951) 253–58.

Tait, Edwin. "A Method for the Christian Life: Martin Bucer and the Sermon on the Mount." PhD diss., Duke University, 2005.

Thompson, Nicholas. *Eucharistic Sacrifice and Patristic Tradition in the Theology of Martin Bucer, 1534–1546*. Leiden: Brill, 2004.

Torrance, Thomas F. *Kingdom and Church: A Study in the Theology of the Reformation*. Edinburgh: Oliver and Boyd, 1956.

Walls, Jerry, ed. *The Oxford Handbook of Eschatology*. Oxford: Oxford University Press, 2008.

Wright, D. F., ed. *Martin Bucer: Reforming Church and Community*. New York: Cambridge University Press, 1994.

Wright, D. F., A. N. Lane, and Jon Balserak, eds. *Calvinus Evangelii Propugnator: Calvin Champion of the Gospel*. Grand Rapids: Calvin Studies Society, 2006.

Zanchius, Jerome, and Augustus Toplady. *The Doctrine of Absolute Predestination Stated and Asserted*. London: George Lindsay, 1811.